GLOBETROTTER

TRAVEL GUIDE

THAILAND

JOHN HOSKIN

NEW
HOLLAND

GLOBETROTTER
TRAVEL GUIDE

First published in 1995 by
New Holland (Publishers) Ltd
London • Cape Town • Sydney • Singapore

Reprinted 1995

ISBN 1 85368 360 4

New Holland (Publishers) Ltd,
24 Nutford Place, London W1H 6DQ

Commissioning Editor: Tim Jollands
Editors: Paul Barnett and Brigitte Lee
Design: Philip Mann, ACE Ltd
Cartography: Globetrotter Travel Maps/ML
Design, London

Typeset by Philip Mann, ACE Ltd
Reproduction by Dot Gradations Ltd, South
Woodham Ferrers
Printed and bound in Hong Kong by South
China Printing Company (1988) Limited

The publishers, author and photographer grate-
fully acknowledge the generous assistance during the compilation of this book of:

The Tourism Authority of Thailand (London
and Bangkok)

Front cover photographs
Top left: *Young Meo woman in Chiang Mai.* **Top
right:** *Buddha statue in a rural setting in Northeast
Thailand.* **Bottom right:** *Floating market at
Damnoen Saduak.* **Bottom left:** *Rafting down the
Ping River, near Chiang Mai.*

Title page photograph
Coastal view of Ko Samui.

CONTENTS

1
Introducing
Thailand

The truth of travel lies in the individual experience, and for most travellers Thailand is an exotic land – with good reason. A distinct culture with a rich and varied heritage remains both visible and accessible, while the natural landscape presents a remarkable range of scenic beauty, from tropical beaches to forested hills. Nowhere else manages quite the same kaleidoscope of sights and scenes.

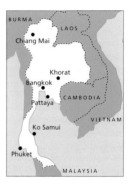

Whenever Thai Airways International takes delivery of a new aircraft, the several million dollars' worth of hi-tech aviation machinery is blessed by a Buddhist monk according to time-honoured ritual. Similarly, soaring Manhattan-style office blocks in Bangkok are inaugurated with propitious rites rooted in ancient beliefs. Any land which can maintain such traditions and host nearly six million visitors a year surely has some magic left to offer.

Throughout its 700 years of independence, the Kingdom has displayed an amazing continuity, underpinned by the peoples' unwavering adherence to Buddhism, the national religion, and to the monarchy which, constitutional since 1932, is as deeply revered now as it was in the days when kings were literally 'Lords of Life'.

Enduring traditions exemplify a quintessential 'Thai-ness' which indelibly colours the nation and gives the sense of an ancient land that is different. Yet the Thais miraculously combine a sincere respect for the past with zest for the new and a joy in today's pleasures.

Opposite: *The very essence of Thailand: gilded spires on Wat Phra Keo, the Temple of the Emerald Buddha in Bangkok.*

It is precisely this seeming paradox that makes Thailand so rewarding. Here is not only a truly multifaceted destination of enormous cultural and topographical diversity, but also all the modern advantages to ensure the most pleasurable travel experience. From exclusive opportunities for sightseeing to excellent accommodation in all categories, superb dining, shopping and leisure, the visitor will find plenty to appreciate.

Thailand's main gateway is **Bangkok**, where most visitors spend at least a few days. The Thai capital can appear confusing and ugly. In what seems variously to be Tokyo, Los Angeles and Disneyland, the skyline is dominated by thrusting highrise blocks, while the constant heat, air pollution and hopeless traffic congestion threaten chaos.

In time, however, negative first impressions fade and Bangkok's inescapable, if idiosyncratic, charm exerts its influence. Within a modern sybaritic world, the city manages to preserve its cultural heritage to a marked degree. The soaring roofs and gleaming spires of the Grand Palace and many historic temples present the visitor with a picture of medieval Oriental wonder, the very stuff of Eastern fairytales.

Beyond Bangkok, tropical beaches are the big attraction. Close to Bangkok is the brash and bawdy international playground of **Pattaya** while, on the opposite shore of the Gulf of Thailand, **Cha-am** and **Hua Hin** provide quieter beach alternatives. Top spots, however, are in the far south, where **Phuket**

Hats and umbrellas: colourful consumer goods for the modern tourist market.

HISTORICAL CALENDAR

6th/7th century Emergence of the Dvaravati kingdom.
660 Establishment by the Mon queen Chama Devi of her capital at Haripunchai.
11th century Khmer empire dominates much of today's eastern and central Thailand.
c1238 Sukhothai founded; inauguration of the Phra Ruang dynasty.
1296 Mengrai establishes the capital of his Lanna kingdom at Chiang Mai.
1350 Ayutthaya founded.
1378 Sukhothai becomes vassal of Ayutthaya (into which it is absorbed 60yr later).
1557 Burma conquers the Lanna kingdom.
1767 Burma conquers Ayutthaya, although triumph is short-lived; new capital

established after the expulsion of the Burmese is Thonburi.
1782 Inauguration of Chakri dynasty with coronation of Rama I; start of Ratanakosin era; adoption of Bangkok as the new capital.
1855 Rama IV (King Mongkut) signs trade agreement with UK, first of a series opening up Siam to the West.
1932 Bloodless revolution; constitutional monarchy inaugurated.
1939 The nation's name is changed from Siam to Thailand.
1942 Thai government led by Field Marshal Phibul Songkhram, keen to cultivate links with Japan, declares war on the UK and USA; this rejected by Thai people and, at WWII's

end, Phibul is deposed.
1946 Rama VIII (King Ananda) found shot dead under circumstances still unexplained; succeeded by his brother, Rama IX (the present King Bhumibol).
1973 Brutal military repression, despite King's intervention, of student unrest.
1974 New civilian constitution declared.
1976 Military resume control after another coup.
1988 Civilian government of Chatichai Choonhaven inaugurated; three years of prosperity ensue, ended by another military coup in 1991.
1992 Massacre by the military at pro-democracy demonstration.

island, **Ko Samui** and **Krabi** boast some of the finest beaches in the world.

By contrast, northern Thailand is an area of uplands with splendid natural scenery and ancient monuments attesting to a long and distinct history. Here the attractions are sightseeing and exploring hill country dotted with the villages of colourful hilltribes.

In between are the Central Plains, the nation's agricultural heartland and site of the ancient capitals of **Ayutthaya** and **Sukhothai**. The area to the west of Bangkok, stretching to the Burmese border, is rich in both history and natural beauty, while Northeast Thailand is the least developed part of the country and in many respects the most traditional.

It is a cliché, but no less true, that Thailand offers something for everyone. It is neither the tropical paradise of tour brochures nor the Sodom and Gomorrah of press reports. Liberally showered with natural gifts and cultural distinctions, Thailand simply presents a rather greater choice than most other places.

FACT FILE

Geography: 1650km (1025 miles) north–south and 800km (500 miles) east–west, with total land area 514,000 sq km (198,475 sq miles). Highest point: Doi Inthanon at 2565m (8415ft).
Government: Constitutional monarchy since 1932. The king is head of state, while legislation is exercised through an elected National Assembly. Thailand is divided into 73 provinces, further subdivided into districts and rural villages.
Population: Nearly 60 million, over 7 million in Bangkok. Ethnic Thais 80%, Chinese 10%, Malay 4%, Khmer, Lao, Vietnamese, hilltribe and others 6%.

THE LAND

In outline, Thailand is fancifully likened to an elephant's head. Bordered in the west by Myanmar (Burma), north by Laos, east by Cambodia and south by Malaysia, Thailand lies roughly midway between India and China, within latitudes 6° and 21° north. The country extends 1650km (1025 miles) north to south, and 800km (500 miles) east to west, but because of the irregular shape, distances between major points are generally comfortable. The land area is 514,000 sq km (198,475 sq miles), roughly the same as that of France. A coastline of more than 2500km (1550 miles) faces the Andaman Sea in the west and the Gulf of Thailand in the east. Several hundred offshore islands, large and small, dot the coastline.

The land divides into six physiographic regions:

The **Central Plains** is an intensely fertile area, comprising the flood plain of the Chao Phraya river, the country's principal waterway, which flows north to south and enters the Gulf of Thailand near Bangkok.

Parallel north–south mountains and fertile valleys define the **North**, which boasts the country's highest peak, Doi Inthanon, at 2565m (8415ft). Main rivers in the North are the Ping, Wang, Yom and Nan, which are the major tributaries of the Chao Phraya.

The **Northeast**, Thailand's poorest and most rural region, occupies the semi-arid Khorat plateau, which is now largely deforested and prone to floods and droughts. The plateau is bordered in the north and east by the Mekong river, which serves as the boundary between Thailand and Laos.

The **East** is a coastal region with many forested offshore islands. Inland from a fertile narrow coastal plain are hills to the west and mountains to the east abutting the Cambodian border.

The **West** is a region of saw-tooth mountains, deflected foothills of the Himalayas. The valleys are smaller than those of the northern highlands and the region is only lightly populated. The main rivers are the Kwai Noi and Kwai Yai, which merge at Kanchanaburi town to form the Mae Khlong river.

The peninsular **South** has an interior of hills (a continuation of the western mountain ranges) and rainforests. A long coastline has fine beaches and many offshore islands along both the western (Andaman Sea) shore and the eastern (Gulf of Thailand) side.

Climate
Thailand has a **tropical** climate with three seasons, although the climatic shifts are not necessarily appreciable to temperate-clime visitors, for whom it may seem hot and humid all year round.

Governing the climate are the alternating southwest and northeast monsoons, steady winds which each blow for roughly six months of the year and so cause wet and dry seasons. The **rainy season** runs from June to October; the (relatively) cool **dry season** lasts from November to February; the **hot season** is from March to May.

Gentle landscape near Chiang Rai in Northern Thailand.

FLORA AND FAUNA
Thailand sustains a wide diversity of flora and fauna. The country's long north–south extent permits an extraordinary range of habitats and climatic zones, from the equatorial to the near-temperate.

If no longer as flourishing as they were, the plant and animal kingdoms are still enormously rich and varied. Estimates reckon that 6% of the world's known species of vascular plants, 10% of the earth's fishes, 10% of the birds, 5% of the reptiles and 3% of the amphibians are found in Thailand. Vegetation includes mangrove swamps, tropical rainforests and pine-clad mountain slopes, while the coastal waters boast a wealth of coral reefs full of marine life.

Although 282 of the world's 4000 mammal species are found in Thailand, creatures of particular note are declining in numbers at an alarming rate. The elephant is most symbolic of the nation, honoured in the past as work animal, war machine and ceremonial figure, though its latter-day fate, too, is sadly representative.

FLORA AND FAUNA

According to the excellent book *National Parks of Thailand*, there are some 15,000 vascular plants native to the country, including more than 500 species of trees and over 1000 orchid varieties. Of Thailand's fauna, birds are the most remarkable with more than 900 recorded species to date. Affording equal opportunity to the naturalist are the country's approximately 1200 types of butterfly.

Vachiratarn waterfall in Doi Inthanon National Park.

The wild elephant population is currently believed to be between 2000 and 3000, and domesticated pachyderms number only slightly more. A century ago there were 20,000 work elephants in Northern Thailand alone.

Other noteworthy indigenous mammals found in varying though again mostly declining numbers include: tigers, leopards, Malayan sun bear, Asiatic black bear, sambar deer, barking deer, mouse deer, gibbons, macaques and various members of the wild cattle family. Reptiles also have their endangered species, especially the river turtle and the freshwater crocodile, which have all but disappeared. Snakes, on the other hand, are well represented in number and species, the latter including six highly venomous varieties. Deadly snakebites are, however, extremely rare.

Thailand's coastal waters provide a rich habitat for marine flora and fauna characteristic of both the Indian Ocean and the Indo-Pacific regions. Game fish include blue marlin, sailfish, barracuda and various types of shark. Coral reefs are also abundant in both the Andaman Sea and the Gulf of Thailand, although the impact of tourism, anchor damage and, most of all, the practice of dynamite fishing have all taken their toll.

National Parks and Conservation

Wonder at the variety of Thailand's flora and fauna must be countered by near despair over environmental deterioration and dwindling wildlife. The situation is most dramatically illustrated by the rate of deforestation. Some 50 years ago about 70% of the country was forested; today, official estimates put forest cover at 25–28%, while most independent observers believe the figure to be less than 20%. The problem has mostly been caused by logging and agriculture. A logging ban was belatedly introduced in 1989, and then only after disastrous mudslides on deforested hills in the south had caused tragic loss of life. But the problem continues: the ban is by no means 100% effective, and commercial reforestation schemes have in many cases done more harm than good.

Wildlife has inevitably suffered from the destruction of natural habitats, and widespread poaching and trade in endangered animals and animal products have made matters worse. All is not gloom, however: although national parks are a comparatively recent

Young girls of the Meo hilltribe in a flower-filled meadow.

development in Thailand (the first, Khao Yai, being established in 1962), the country now boasts 63 parks and 32 wildlife sanctuaries which together cover 11% of the total land area – a higher than average proportion.

To what degree these areas are protected is a moot point: poaching and land encroachment are persistent problems. On a positive note, the public apathy and ignorance of just over a decade ago is giving way to ever greater concern and, more importantly, action regarding environmental issues.

National Park Highlights

Khao Yai: Some of the richest remaining rainforest in Asia lies within the boundary of Thailand's oldest and most visited national park, roughly midway between Bangkok and Khorat. The park covers an area of 2172 sq km (840 sq miles) and is crossed by over 50km (31 miles) of hiking trails. (See page 80.)

Erawan: Set in the valley of the Kwai Yai 72 km (45 miles) north of Kanchanaburi town, this attractive park has forest trails and beautiful waterfalls. (See page 52.)

Doi Inthanon: Some 80km (50 miles) southwest of Chiang Mai, Thailand's highest peak is situated in an area designated as a national park. Typical northern countryside, picturesque waterfalls and hilltribe villages are the principal attractions. (See page 70.)

Phu Kradung: Situated 80km (50 miles) south of Loei town, this picturesque plateau at an average elevation of 1300m (4265ft) has an area of 60 sq km (23 sq miles) covered in savanna and lofty pines. (See page 85.)

Ko Samet: This island retreat some 6km (4 miles) off the coast from Ban Phe in Rayong province is officially designated as a national park. Its main attractions are its secluded coves, fine sandy beaches and coral reefs. (See page 94.)

Khao Sam Roi Yot: South of Hua Hin, the 'Mountain of 300 Peaks' national park covers an area of 100 sq km (38 sq miles) and is composed of a series of monumental limestone outcrops forming the habitat of numerous species of shore birds. There are stunning panoramic views of the southern coastline. (See page 102.)

Wat Arun, the 'Temple of the Dawn', in Bangkok.

HISTORY IN BRIEF

Known as Siam until 1939, Thailand has a history as a sovereign state dating back more than 700 years. The modern name means literally 'Land of the Free', and although this sounds suspiciously trite the Thais have experienced exceptional historical freedom. Unlike its neighbours, Thailand never suffered the fate of colonization by a European power.

Pre-Thai Era

Knowledge of the prehistory of the area is still scant, though it appears that the earliest inhabitants were displaced by diverse waves of immigration until, ultimately, the Thais, originally from what is now part of southern China, became dominant. Prior to their ascendancy, however, various influences were at work.

Fundamental to the development of Southeast Asia was the impact of ancient India. Stimulated by a kind of cultural osmosis effected during the first centuries AD, whereby aspects of Indian civilization were acquired, a number of indigenous independent kingdoms arose. Three were especially formative on what would later become Thailand.

The first, **Dvaravati**, was a vaguely united group of Mon people settled in a collection of city states with, most likely, a power base at what is now Nakhon Pathom, west of Bangkok. The Dvaravati kingdom flourished in the Chao Phraya river basin from the 6th or 7th to the 11th century. It embraced Theravada Buddhism; it is generally assumed the Thais were initially converted to the faith through contact with the Mon.

The second formative kingdom was that of **Sriwijaya**, an approximate contemporary of Dvaravati which held sway in the Malay peninsula and Indonesian archipelago from the 8th to the late 13th century. Sriwijaya moulded the early culture of southern Thailand.

The third and most influential was the kingdom of the **Khmer**, whose vast empire was centred on Angkor.

By the 11th century the Khmer dominated not only what is now Cambodia but also large tracts of eastern and central present-day Thailand. They were master builders and traces of their achievement are still readily discernible in Lop Buri and various sites in the Northeast.

Sukhothai

By the early 13th century the power of the Khmer was waning while the Thais, who had been migrating steadily southwards from China, were gaining strength and setting up small autonomous settlements. In c1238 the chieftains of two such Thai groups united their forces and founded the first sovereign Thai capital at Sukhothai. One of the chieftains, Phor Khun Bang Klang Thao, was proclaimed king, taking the title Sri Intradit and establishing the first Thai dynasty, **Phra Ruang**.

Gradually Sukhothai exerted its influence and during the third reign, that of King Ramkamhaeng (c1279–99), the kingdom was consolidated, politically through territorial gains and culturally through the adoption of Theravada Buddhism; strong links were established with neighbouring China, and extensive trading relations with Cambodia and India. A cultural flowering came during the reign of King Lithai (1347–c68), when distinctive Thai art and architectural styles achieved their first – and, some say, their finest – expression.

Ayutthaya

Founded by King U Thong (later crowned Ramathibodi) in 1368, Ayutthaya rapidly gained power and, after absorbing Sukhothai, remained the heart of the Thai state for the next 400 years, exercising control over virtually all Thai territory except the North.

After territorial expansion in the 15th century, the 1500s witnessed a succession of wars, mainly against Burma, which defeated Ayutthaya in 1569. Only 15 years later, however, King Naresuan the Great not only defeated the Burmese but also succeeded in pushing his national borders even further than before.

Ayutthaya's glory peaked in the 17th century, most

Wat Sra Sri, sited on an island in Sukhothai Historical Park.

SUKHOTHAI

As the undisputed centre of the new Thai nation, Sukhothai reigned supreme for only 140 years. In 1378 it became a vassal of another, younger Thai state, that of Ayutthaya to the south, and 60 years later was totally absorbed by this second Thai kingdom. Yet in its brief span Sukhothai established religious, cultural and political patterns which formed a lasting framework for Thai society.

View of Wat Phra Keo, the Temple of the Emerald Buddha, across the Chao Phraya river, Bangkok.

spectacularly during the reign of King Narai the Great (1656–88). Aided by his colourful first minister, a wily Greek known as Phaulkon, he attempted an alliance with the French, but was ultimately defeated by conservative elements at court who compounded international intrigues of Byzantine complexity. He was lucky to die a natural death; the French were unceremoniously expelled from the country.

In 1767 that perennial enemy, Burma, made an all-out attack and after a lengthy siege captured Ayutthaya, systematically looted it, killed or took off into slavery all but 10,000 inhabitants and razed the city. Ferocious though this attack was, the invaders were unable to consolidate territorial gains. The Thais quickly rallied under General Taksin, who had established a resistance base at Thonburi on the opposite bank of the Chao Phraya river from Bangkok. Before the close of the year that had seen the destruction of Ayutthaya, he had established a new capital, Thonburi, had been crowned king and had begun to reunite the people.

The Kingdom of Lanna

Running parallel to the history of Sukhothai and Ayutthaya is that of the Lanna kingdom, which ruled the mountain valleys of the North. This was also a Thai state, friend of Sukhothai but foe of Ayutthaya, and maintained a largely separate development until the modern era.

The earliest inhabitants of the North were probably the Lawa, who were subsequently forced into the highlands when the valleys were taken over by lowland people. First came an offshoot of the Mons, led by a legendary queen, Chama Devi, who founded a capital in AD660 at Haripunchai, present-day Lamphun.

Later, migrating Thais settled in parts of the North, setting up petty city states. By the 13th century the most powerful of these was Chiang Saen, on the banks of the Mekong river, and in 1259 its ruler, King Mengrai, set about exerting his control over neighbouring Thai principalities. Through patience and guile, he eventually became ruler of a state he was to call Lanna, meaning 'a million rice fields', for which he built a new capital, Chiang Mai, in 1296. By the time he died in 1317, reputedly struck by lightning, he had brought much of what is now northern Thailand into one fold, Lanna, with Chiang Mai as its power base.

Immediate successors were kings of lesser stature and there were some troubled times, but the power of Lanna became such as to attract the hostile interest of Ayutthaya. A see-saw kind of conflict persisted between Lanna and Ayutthaya from the mid-15th century onwards. This did not prevent Chiang Mai from experiencing its golden age during the reign of King Tilokaraja (1442–87). He fought to a stalemate with Ayutthaya's equally forceful King Trailok, but scored notable successes elsewhere, conquering the state of Nan in 1449. He was also a stalwart upholder of Buddhism and a patron of the arts, and several distinguished Chiang Mai temples and Buddha sculptures date from his reign.

In 1557 Lanna was conquered by the Burmese. Independence was lost for the next two centuries. The form of the eclipse, however, was erratic: sometimes there were puppet Lanna kings; at other times there was direct rule from Burma. This state of affairs persisted until the late 18th century when King Taksin succeeded in expelling the Burmese from all Thai territory. Lanna, although now part of the Thai fold, retained a certain autonomy under a line of hereditary rulers until the early 20th century when the central government assumed direct rule.

A statue of the Buddha in the ruined ancient capital, Ayutthaya.

Opposite: *The National Assembly, Bangkok.*

Below: *Courtyard in the Royal Summer Palace at Bang Pa-In.*

The Ratanakosin Era

The modern period, the Ratanakosin era, begins with the founding of Bangkok as the capital in 1782. Although King Taksin from his capital at Thonburi had led the Thais to a remarkable recovery from the Burmese invasion and had largely reunified the nation, his reign was short-lived. By 1782 he had reputedly become insane and was overthrown in a coup and executed. The Commander of the Army, General Chakri, was then popularly proclaimed King, being crowned Rama I and so founding the **Chakri dynasty** which reigns to this day. One of his first acts was to transfer his power base across the Chao Phraya river from Thonburi to Bangkok, at the time little more than a customs post and a huddle of Chinese traders' huts. The reason for the move was partly symbolic as Rama I wished to restore national pride by constructing a city that would recreate the lost glory of Ayutthaya.

During the first three reigns of the Chakri dynasty, Bangkok was transformed from a riverside village into an impressive capital. The construction of canals effectively turned it into an island city, while the

building of the Grand Palace, the Temple of the Emerald Buddha and the other buildings which today constitute Bangkok's major sights successfully reflected material and spiritual wealth.

The pattern of development shifted with the succession of King Mongkut, Rama IV, in 1851. The idea of recreating Ayutthaya was abandoned, along with the nation's introspective stance. Mongkut had

spent 27 years in the monkhood and had proved himself a scholar of considerable attainment. As an enlightened monarch possessed of an intelligent and inquiring mind, he was to set the country on a path of modernization by opening the door to Western influence.

The first major step was taken in 1855 when he signed a mutually favourable trade agreement with Sir John Bowring, envoy of Queen Victoria. Similar accords with other European countries and with the USA followed in quick succession. In tandem with expanding international trade, the country embarked upon a programme of modernization of far-reaching proportions. Infrastructure was expanded and developed to meet new needs (notably, roads for wheeled traffic began to replace canals), and the machinery of state was overhauled with ministries organized along European lines. Art and architecture also began to reflect an interest in things Western, as can be noticed today in Bangkok's several Italianate buildings of the period, such as the former National Assembly.

MASTER OF ITS OWN DESTINY

The absence of imperialism allowed Chinese migrants, who were to play a vital role in the development of business and commerce, to be well assimilated into mainstream Thai society. US academic Charles F. Keyes wrote: 'Although Siamese society, with its large Chinese migrant population, was in some ways similar to the societies of other Southeast Asian nations because of its incorporation into an international economic system, in other fundamental ways it evolved differently because, unlike those other societies, it was transformed politically by an indigenous elite rather than by Western colonial rulers.'

Mongkut's son and successor, King Chulalongkorn (reigned 1868–1910), furthered the policies of modernization. He successfully introduced various sweeping reforms, including the abolition of slavery, and broadly adopted European concepts of administration, justice, education and public welfare. In the following reign, that of King Vajiravudh (1910–25), compulsory education was established, among other developments. On the international front, Vajiravudh, who had been educated in the UK, brought Thailand into World War I on the side of the Allies.

With such fundamental change and material development it was almost inevitable that traditional concepts of power would be questioned. For centuries Thai kings had been literally 'Lords of Life', but that ended in 1932 when a bloodless revolution changed the system of government to a constitutional monarchy. The reigning monarch, King Prajadhipok (reigned 1925–35), accepted a *fait accompli*, though he abdicated to be succeeded by his nephew, King Ananda.

In the present era, Thailand has moved slowly and, at times, with difficulty towards establishing an effective democracy. Since 1932 the constitution has been changed many times, and military coups, successful and abortive, were until recently frequent occurrences. But although the peaceful evolution of popular government has been disturbed, it has not been halted.

Traditional Thai pavilion in the gardens of the Suan Pakkard Palace, Bangkok.

Throughout, the monarchy has had a valuable stabilizing effect. After King Ananda's tragic death in 1946, his brother, the present King Bhumibol Adulyadej, Rama IX, succeeded to the throne. King Bhumibol has shown himself to be the model of a modern constitutional monarch, both preserving regal traditions and taking an active part in working towards the greater social and economic well-being of his people.

GOVERNMENT AND ECONOMY

Thailand is governed by a constitutional monarchy, with a **prime minister**, an elected 360-seat **lower house** and an **upper house** of 270 appointed senators. There are similarities with the UK system, although the Thai monarchy remains more influential, in both an advisory capacity and through practical development projects initiated by the **King** and other members of the **Royal Family**.

Ostensibly within the constitutional framework, the **military** has traditionally been a powerful force in politics, staging numerous coups, the most recent in 1991. There are indications, however, that moves towards true democracy are beginning to gain ground: although a pro-democracy demonstration was bloodily suppressed by the military in May 1992, the event did succeed in raising public commitment to democracy, while the military was reflected in a poor light.

In administrative terms, Thailand is divided into 73 **provinces**, each with a governor and provincial capital city. The next subdivision is that of **district**, while the traditional social and administrative base is the rural **village**, where authority is popularly invested in a village headman.

Rapid material gains have been made in the last decade and Bangkok's bristling highrise skyline is the most obvious outward sign of an unprecedented economic boom. The annual economic growth rate has averaged just over 7% since 1986, a performance unrivalled by Thailand's neighbours, and the nation is now poised to assume NIC (newly industrialized country) status. This rapid economic growth has stressed the nation's infrastructure to the limit, and solutions to such problems are not readily visible.

Thailand's single largest foreign-exchange earner is tourism. A 'Visit Thailand Year' promotion brought in a then record 3.5 million visitors in 1987. The figure is now well over five million, and in spite of disappointing performances in the early 1990s, sustained growth is expected.

SUCCESS STORY

Spearheading Thailand's economic boom has been a dynamic export drive. **Agriculture**, the traditional source of income, remains strong enough to ensure Thailand's ranking as the world's fifth largest food exporter. However, its performance has been outstripped by **manufacturing**. Today, not only does the world buy most of its rice, tapioca and tinned pineapples from the Kingdom, it is also shopping increasingly for made-in-Thailand shoes, garments, jewellery and other manufactured items. Overall, manufactured goods account for 60% of Thailand's exports. In 1960 the figure stood at a minute 2.4%.

THE PEOPLE

The population of Thailand is approaching 60 million, of which just over 10% live in Bangkok. The growth rate is currently less than 1.5%.

Ethnic Thais account for the majority of the population, although there are several regional subdivisions, each having their own dialect – Thai Yai (Shan) in the Northwest, Pak Thai in the South, Thai-Lao and Thai Khorat in the Northeast, among others. As a result of various migratory patterns in the past, Chinese, Malay, Mon, Khmer, Burmese and Indian ethnic strains are also found in varying degrees throughout Thailand. Assimilation of the main minorities is almost total. Other distinct minorities – various northern tribal people, Khmer, Lao and Vietnamese refugees and a small foreign community – account for less than 10% of the population.

About 60% of the people continue to derive a living directly or indirectly from the land. The rural village tied to the agricultural cycle remains an important social unit, and middle-class urban culture is only now developing.

With a population of at least seven million, Bangkok is by far the largest city, and the biggest towns – Khon

Woman of the Akha hill-tribe of Northern Thailand.

Kaen, Chiang Mai, Khorat, Hat Yai – scarcely number more than 200,000 inhabitants. All major administrative, financial, industrial and commercial activity is concentrated in the capital. The pattern is slowly shifting, with tentative moves towards decentralization.

In terms of national traits, Thailand has been dubbed 'The Land of Smiles', and it is true that the people are essentially hospitable, fun-loving and easy-going – *mai pen rai*, meaning 'it doesn't matter', is one common Thai phrase everyone soon learns. But the national character is rooted in adherence to traditional values resulting in a well developed sense of national identity and pride.

RELIGION

Throughout the history of the Kingdom, **Buddhism** has been Thailand's national religion and its impact is all-embracing. It is professed and practised by nine-tenths of the population, while gilded temple spires, ubiquitous Buddha statues and files of saffron-robed monks on morning alms rounds are all distinctive images of Thai life.

One of the world's great living religions, Buddhism is, strictly speaking, atheistic in that it neither implies any question of faith nor demands any belief in the existence of a god. Essentially, it is a rational philosophy, derived from the teachings of the Buddha, the 'Enlightened One', the title of a historical person, Siddhartha Gautama. The Buddha was born around 560BC near present-day Lumbini in southern Nepal. He spent his long life – he died in his 80th year – teaching around the central region of the Ganges plain, gathering a large number of followers. Disciples were encouraged to take full responsibility for their thoughts and actions on a path to spiritual growth that was in essence a way of life rather than an organized religion. Some of the Buddha's followers did none the less become ordained and formed the monkhood (*sangha*) in which they lived disciplined lives and sought wisdom, their prime virtue. The early form of Buddhism, known as **Theravada** or the 'teaching of the elders', was later challenged by a new

MONKS AND MONASTERIES

The monastic system is central to Theravada Buddhism and in Thailand today there are at any one time some 250,000 Buddhist monks residing at an estimated 27,000 temple monasteries throughout the country. Aside from a core religious community, most monks are ordained for only a short spell, perhaps just a few days, but more usually for the three months of the Buddhist Rains Retreat. As in the past, young Thai men become monks temporarily to earn merit for their parents as well as for their own spiritual development.

SPIRIT HOUSES

The Thai belief in spirits is most graphically illustrated by the spirit houses found in the compounds of virtually all homes, business premises, government offices and public buildings. These small, highly ornate structures, usually in the form of a temple or traditional Thai house, are meant as dwellings for the spirits which originally occupied the land and have been displaced by the human tenants. Not only must the spirits be given a house, they must also be placated with food and other offerings lest their displeasure is incurred, bringing misfortune.

school which aimed to have a more popular appeal. It called itself **Mahayana**, or 'Great Vehicle', as it offered salvation to a greater number of people than Theravada Buddhism, which it derisively termed Hinayana, or 'Small Vehicle'.

Though sharing basic doctrines with Theravada Buddhism, the Mahayana school places less emphasis on monasticism and claims any layman may achieve *nirvana*, release from the individual's endless cycle of reincarnation and suffering by extinguishing desire. It also differs in considering the Buddha omnipresent, representing not only the Enlightened One but also the principle of Enlightenment. Mahayana further introduces the concept of Bodhisattvas, Enlightened beings who decline entering *nirvana* in order to help others. In this way the religion evolved into a theistic faith, with the divine radiance of the Buddha emanating from heaven, and man benefiting from the compassion of deities and Bodhisattvas; but it was Theravada Buddhism that became the dominant faith in Thailand. In trying to lead a good life the layman has the opportunity to accrue merit by, for example, giving food and other offerings to monks who make early morning alms rounds in cities, towns and villages throughout the country. This will ensure rebirth under more favourable conditions in the next incarnation.

Wat Chang Lom, a late-13th-century temple at the historic site of Si Satchanalai in the Central Plains.

Pervasive and genuine though their adherence to Buddhism is, the Thais have retained from their ancestors **animistic** practices which interact with ordinary life. These include beliefs in charms, amulets, magical tattoos, fortune telling, exorcism and other shamanistic rituals, as well as in spirits. Similarly, **Brahmanism**, the ancient form of Hinduism which was a potent influence on the early development of Southeast Asian civilization, also continues to play an important role in rituals, notably in traditional royal ceremonies.

ARTS AND CULTURE

Classical Thai art has been almost exclusively produced in the service of Theravada Buddhism, and it is the Thai temple that both defines the culture and provides a showcase of sculpture, painting and the decorative arts. Temples are rightly at the top of any sightseeing list, and a little understanding of their form and significance helps an appreciation of Thailand's artistic heritage.

The word 'temple' is largely unsatisfactory as a translation of the Thai word *wat*. It implies a single structure, as is the case with a Christian church, but this is not so with a Buddhist *wat*. Besides monks' residential quarters, which are commonly, though not always, found at a *wat*, a Thai temple complex comprises several distinct religious buildings.

The principal structure is the *bot*, the most sacred part of the temple and the place where ordination ceremonies are conducted. The building is identified by eight boundary stones, called *sima*, placed outside at the four corners and the four cardinal points.

A temple will probably also have at least one *viharn*, a hall virtually identical to a *bot* but without the *sima*. This building is used as a sermon hall for monks and lay worshippers. Both the *viharn* and the *bot*

Young Buddhist monks at a temple compound shrine in East Thailand.

> **RELIGIOUS ART**
>
> Images of the Buddha were executed in one of four basic postures – standing, sitting, walking and reclining. In addition, individual images display different *mudras*, or hand gestures. For example, both hands placed in the lap of the sitting Buddha indicate the meditation pose, whereas if the fingers of the right hand are pointing to the ground the statue represents the Buddha's subduing of Mara (forces of evil). In the standing image, the right hand raised signifies the *mudra* of 'Dispelling Fear'

KEY STAGES OF THAI ART

Dvaravati (6th–11th centuries): Indian-influenced style originally propagated by the Mons. Architecture characterized by brick and laterite with stucco decorative elements, although there are few extant remains.

Sriwijaya (8th–13th centuries) held sway in the Malay peninsula and Indonesian archipelago and as far as the Nakhon Si Thammarat region in Southern Thailand. Notable for its sculpture, especially free-standing stone pieces.

Lop Buri (7th–14th centuries): School flourished when the region was controlled by the Khmers, master builders who left traces of their achievements in Lop Buri and various sites in the Northeast. Architecture shows harmony and elegance.

Sukhothai (late 13th–15th centuries): Marks emergence of a specifically Thai art. The Buddha has long earlobes, beaked nose and serene smile.

Lanna (11th–13th centuries): Particularly associated with Northern Thailand during the Sukhothai period. Structures often used wood, so very few original buildings remain. Buddha statuettes were sculpted in semi-precious stone.

U Thong (12th–15th centuries): Influenced by Khmer art until 13th century. Buddha usually wears a head-band and is depicted in the attitude of subduing Mara.

Ayutthaya (15th–18th centuries): Lacquerwork and murals show a preoccupation with ornament, and classical statuary is rich in decoration.

enshrine Buddha statues, a presiding image and commonly several smaller attendant statues. Many of these images are of great antiquity, and some possess individual fame, revered as possessing unusual spiritual power.

Both *bot* and *viharn* follow identical architectural styles, being rectangular buildings with sweeping multi-tiered roofs covered with glazed brown and green or blue tiles. Each end of the roof's peak terminates in a gilded finial known as a *cho fa*, or 'sky tassel'. A gracefully curved ornamentation, it looks like a slender bird's neck and head, and is generally believed to represent the mythical *garuda*, half bird, half man.

Along with the *bot* and *viharn*, the most characteristic of temple structures is the *chedi* or *stupa*. Dominating the compound of a *wat*, this is a tall decorative spire constructed over relics of the Buddha, sacred texts or an image. Essentially, they are of two basic forms: bell-shaped, raised on square or round terraces of diminishing size and tapering to a thin spire, or a round, finger-like tower. The latter, derived from Khmer architecture and symbolic of the mythical mountain abode of the gods, is known as a *prang*.

Other buildings in a temple compound can include a library for sacred texts, and a *mondop*. Traditionally the former was built on stilts over a pond to protect the fragile manuscripts from ants. The *mondop* is a square-shaped building with tapering roof enshrining some relic, often a Buddha footprint, a decorated stone impression far larger than lifesize. These, like the *chedi*, are not merely architectural features; they also serve as monuments in the true sense, objects to instruct and focus the mind.

Some larger *wats* may also have cloisters, open-sided galleries perhaps displaying rows of Buddha images, while bell towers and various pavilions can be additional features. *Wats* further have a crematorium, identified by its needle-like chimney, and, usually, a school for monks and perhaps also for lay children.

Most fascinating from the visitor's point of view is

the temple as art centre. Unlike the *wat*'s other functions, this role was unwittingly assumed. Until the modern period all Thai art was religious art: it had no conscious aesthetic function and served purely didactic and devotional aims. Thus sculpture, painting and the minor arts, such as gilt on lacquer, mother-of-pearl inlay and woodcarving, found expression almost exclusively in temple decoration.

Sculpture was largely limited to images of the Buddha. These are not idols but rather reminders of the teachings and, in theory at least, are all modelled on the same attributes of the Enlightened One. In practice, of course, sculpture did develop different styles during various art periods and Buddha statues do vary considerably in form and expression.

The *wat* is also a showcase of Thai classical painting, the artform achieving its finest expression in murals. Typically these were painted on all four walls of *bots* and *viharns*, though owing to the fragile nature of the medium and the ravages of the climate, few surviving examples predate the 18th century.

All murals were purely didactic in purpose and the classic formula was to decorate the side walls with episodes from the life of the Buddha or his previous incarnations, individual scenes being separated by registers of praying celestial beings. The back wall generally showed a graphic interpretation of the Buddhist cosmology, and the front wall was covered with the scene of Buddha's victory over Mara (forces of evil). Typically, murals lack any attempt at perspective and figures tend to be small, while the entire picture area is filled with detail. Because of the latter convention, artists often completed backgrounds with scenes and episodes from Thai daily life. These are fascinating both for their content and as areas where the painters display greater self-expression.

Doors and window shutters also sometimes have painted scenes, while all flat surfaces are commonly brilliantly adorned. Especially notable among the decorative arts are mother-of-pearl inlay and gilt on

Intricately carved doorway at Wat Pumin in Nan, North Thailand.

Scene from one of the fine murals covering the interior walls of Wat Pumin.

THE ART OF *KHON*

Traditionally, *khon* dances were solely royal court entertainments and were performed by an all-male cast with a story-line taken exclusively from the *Ramakien* epic. Today, girls may play the female roles. Distinctive masks are worn by all but the lead dancers, whose person-alities are subordinated by heavy make-up and elaborate costumes. Gestures are highly stylized, each with its own sig-nificance. In the past, perfor-mances could last all day, but in modern times it is normal to present only the most popular episodes from the *Ramakien*.

lacquer work, which frequently have a high pictorial quality. Coloured-glass mosaic is also quite often used and adds to a temple's lavish overall decoration.

Also to be seen in temple compounds are statues of various mythological beings. While high-art sculpture was limited to images of the Buddha, craftsmen had scope in creating minor statuary, representations of creatures which play familiar roles in Thai myths and legends. Among those most commonly seen are the *garuda*, the mount of the god Vishnu; the *naga*, king of serpents, frequently fashioned in the form of balustrades flanking stairways at temple entrances; *yakshas*, giants charged with guarding a temple against evil spirits; *kinnaris*, graceful beings half woman and half bird; and *apsaras*, or celestial nymphs, who dance for the delight of the gods.

Solid gold Buddha in Wat Traimit, on the fringe of Bangkok's Chinatown.

Performing Arts

Outside the religious context, Thailand has a long tradition of performing arts. Puppet and shadow theatre

can occasionally be seen, but it is classical dance which is best preserved.

The two major forms of Thai classical dance drama are *khon* and *lakon nai*. Both were originally exclusively court entertainments and it was not until much later that a popular style of dance theatre, *likay*, evolved as a diversion for the common folk. To draw parallels with Western dance and drama, *likay* is the equivalent of pantomime, whereas *khon* and *lakon nai* are like ballet, classical and highly stylized.

The visitor can most easily see classical dance at one of the several dinner-shows staged at various Bangkok restaurants, although it should be remembered that these programmes mix the classical with the folk and present perhaps a ten-minute excerpt of *khon* or *lakon nai*. More traditional performances are staged at Bangkok's National Theatre. *Likay* shows are most likely to be seen at temple fairs and at upcountry festivals.

The traditional Lantern Dance performed during the Loy Krathong festival.

Sports and Recreation

Kick boxing – *Muay Thai* – is traditionally Thailand's most popular spectator sport. Developed from an ancient style of martial art, *Muay Thai* differs from ordinary boxing in that the feet, knees and elbows are used as weapons in addition to gloved fists. At its best it is a fast and furious contest between two superbly fit athletes.

Among other violent sports are Thai **sword fighting** (*krabi-krabong*) and improbable animal contests: bull fighting (bull against bull, not the Spanish variety), fish fighting, cock fighting (which is illegal), and even beetle fighting.

Also very Thai but far less violent is **takraw**, a game somewhat akin to volleyball in which a rattan ball is knocked around by using the feet, legs and head only. A recognized sport at national and regional meets, *takraw* is most commonly seen being played by young men during their lunch break on any open space.

Tourists on an elephant ride in Bangkok's Rose Garden.

Of modern sports, **golf** is rapidly becoming Thailand's most popular pastime. The country boasts a surprising number of splendid courses. Most popular with visitors are a host of **watersports**. Much of Thailand's long coastline is unspoilt, and deserted islands, coral reefs and sheer cliffs provide an attractive backdrop for scuba diving, snorkelling, yachting, windsurfing, water-skiing, deep-sea fishing and sea canoeing.

Trekking and **mountain biking** are dry-land adventure-sports options. The hill country of the North is ideally suited to both, and organized tours are readily available.

WHERE TO EAT IN THAILAND

The choice of where to eat is as wide as that of what to eat. Restaurants in all categories from inexpensive cafés to smart establishments abound in Bangkok and other major cities. When travelling, the best rule of thumb is to eat where you see the locals eating. Don't be shy of the ubiquitous kerbside stalls selling noodle dishes and other Oriental 'fast foods'. These are good, inexpensive, and generally safe in spite of appearances.

LUSCIOUS FRUITS

Durian: A huge, spiky fruit renowned for its sewer-like stench and its sweet custardy taste.
Kluai khai farang: 'Foreign banana', a plump, cylindrical version of the well known fruit.
Lamut: Light-brown fruit that has to be peeled, with a syrup-sweet taste reminiscent of figs.
Ngor: Rambutan; a small, hairy outer casing conceals the tiny fruit.
Sapparod: Pineapple, ten times tastier on its home territory.
Somo: Pomelo, a tropical relation of the grapefruit.

Sifting cashew nuts laid out to dry in the sun in southern Thailand.

FOOD AND DRINK

Thai food is enormously rich in variety and piquant in taste, and most visitors quickly come to share the Thais' high regard for the national fare.

Pork and poultry are favoured meats, although many types of fish and shellfish, both freshwater and from the sea, are a traditional source of protein and are equally popular, more so in some regions. But the basis of a Thai meal is rice. This is commonly steamed, although it may be made into noodles, while glutinous or 'sticky' rice is preferred with some regional specialities. Accompanying the rice are four or five main dishes featuring vegetables, meat, seafood, fish, eggs and soup according to choice. Utensils are a fork and spoon; after helping yourself to a scoop of rice, you take small amounts from the other dishes as taste and appetite dictate.

Besides the rice and main dishes, essential to any Thai meal are the sauces. There are a staggering number, but the commonest are *nam pla*, a liquid fish sauce which is extremely salty, and *nam prik*, also liquid but with pieces of chillies, garlic, shrimp curd, sugar and lime.

Thailand's great contribution to the culinary arts is *tom yam*, a sour soup which can be made with various kinds

of meat or fish; its most famous version is with prawns, *tom yam goong*. The basic broth is flavoured with lemon grass, citrus leaves, lime juice, fish sauce and hot chillies.

Other common methods of Thai food preparation include curries (*gaeng*), usually hot and spicy, and the stir-fried dishes which are cooked in a wok with pork fat oil, pepper and plenty of garlic. There is a wide choice of salad preparations (*yam*) made with just vegetables or with different kinds of meat or fish mixed with distinctive flavourings like lemon grass and fish sauce, together with lime juice for characteristic tartness.

For dessert there are many sorts of local sweets (*kanom*), often flavoured with coconut and very sugary, as well as a bewildering choice of tropical fruits, including the sweet-tasting but foul-smelling durian, luscious mangosteens, rambutans and custard apples.

Northeastern Thailand possesses a regional cuisine that has become extremely popular in recent years. It features a wide variety of exotic ingredients, among them frogs and grasshoppers, and uses chilli peppers to a greater degree than elsewhere in Thailand. Among typical Northeastern dishes are green papaya salad (*som tam*) and spicy minced meat or chicken, known as *larb*.

DRINKS

Beer is a good (though comparatively expensive) complement to Thai food, and is available in three local brands: Singha, Kloster and Amarit. Strongest is Singha at 4.6%, but Kloster and Amarit at 4% are still heady brews. All are lagers though there are marked differences in taste; Singha, for example, has a distinctly more malty flavour.

Typically Thai are various local **spirits**, the most famous of which is **Mekong rice whisky**. Distilled from molasses and sticky rice in a month-long process, Mekong is 35% alcohol (70 proof) and has a slightly coarse flavour which is an acquired taste. Unlike scotch or bourbon, Mekong cannot really be drunk neat and is best taken as a long drink with plenty of water or soda and lots of ice. Like beer, Mekong goes extremely well with virtually any type of Thai food.

Non-alcoholic beverages include **fresh fruit juices** and familiar brands of soft drink. Avoid drinking excessive quantities of fruit juice when you are very hot and never drink tap water. Bottled local **mineral water** is good and readily available.

Typical Thai open-fronted shops piled high with produce.

2
Bangkok

Bangkok is not a beautiful city, nor at first glance is it obviously Oriental. But it is unquestionably captivating, exerting an irresistible charm as the epitome of all things Thai.

Alec Waugh captured its essence perfectly in his book on the Thai capital: 'Bangkok has been loved,' he wrote, 'because it is an expression of the Thais themselves, of their lightheartedness, their love of beauty, their reverence for tradition, their sense of freedom, their extravagance, their devotion to their creed – to characteristics that are constant and continuing in themselves.'

In its contradictory impulses towards love for the old and lust for the new, Bangkok is a huge paradox. Hence the madcap mix of gorgeous temples and glitzy department stores, of serene Buddha images and snarling traffic, of religious devotion and sensual pleasure, of cultural refinement and modern chaos. Yet above all it is the Thais' exceptional tolerance that gives the city a real sense of freedom.

Sprawling over a flat alluvial plain, stretching back from the banks of the **Chao Phraya river** some 40km (25 miles) from its mouth on the Gulf of Thailand, Bangkok is a confusing city. The unrelieved flatness of the location permits virtually no topographical distinction, while the city itself lacks any single central area. The Chao Phraya divides the city into Bangkok proper, on the east bank, and **Thonburi** (now part of the metropolitan area) on the west. Otherwise Bangkok comprises a cluster of districts with no obvious logical connection.

Opposite: *The bustling city of Bangkok contains a chaotic mix of ancient and modern.*

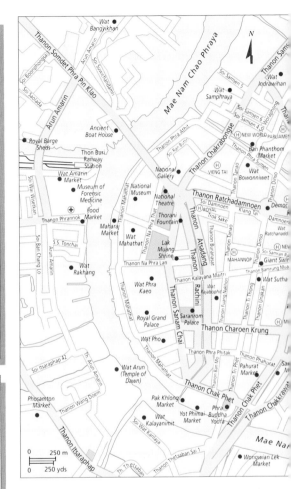

The original city centre, the old royal city, lies on the east bank of the Chao Phraya, its borders defined by the river and Krung Kasem road and canal, the latter connecting with the Chao Phraya and forming what is sometimes called **Ratanakosin Island**. Immediately north is the **Dusit** area, the 'new' royal city where the official royal residence, **Chitralada Palace**, is located.

Extending southeast and then south of Ratanakosin

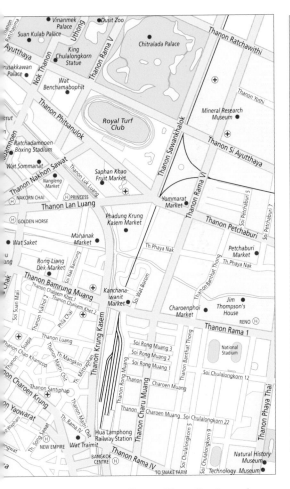

BACKGROUND IN BRIEF

Bangkok is comparatively youthful. A riverine village and customs post until the late 18th century, it was founded as the national capital in 1782 by King Rama I. Initially intended to parallel the lost glory of Ayutthaya, Bangkok was developed as an island city with a web of canals. Palaces and temples in classical architecture were the only substantial buildings; houses and other structures were made of wood.

Change came in the mid-19th century when King Mongkut, Rama VI, ordered the building of the first roads for wheeled traffic. In the same reign, Bangkok was launched on the path of commerce with the signing of international trade agreements. A pattern of modernization and commercialization along largely Western lines has been followed ever since.

Today most of the canals have been filled in to make way for roads, and the city has expanded far away from the Chao Phraya river, thereby losing its original focal point and abandoning any semblance of a downtown area.

Island is **New Road** (Charoen Krung Road – no longer 'new' but Bangkok's first proper road) which cuts through the old trade quarter of **Chinatown**.

To the south is the **Silom** area, a business, shopping and tourist district where you'll find clusters of delightful street stalls, while to the east, beyond Rama VI Road, are the **Ploenchit** and **Sukhumvit** areas, mixing commercial and residential.

OLD ROYAL CITY – TOUR 1

Bangkok's original heart contains the greatest concentration of historic monuments. Described below are the principal sights as encountered on two possible walking tours. In keeping with what was once the 'Venice of the East', old Bangkok is most appropriately approached via the Chao Phraya, and so our tour begins by taking a river taxi to the Tha Tien landing stage, adjacent to Wat Po.

Wat Po, Temple of the Reclining Buddha ***

Open daily 08:00–17:00. Properly called Wat Phra Chetupon, Wat Po is Bangkok's oldest and largest temple/monastery complex and, arguably, the single most fascinating. It dates from the 16th century, although it was radically remodelled and enlarged in 1789 by King Rama I and further renovated in succeeding reigns.

With a compound packed with chapels, pavilions, *chedis*, Buddha images and a profusion of other statuary, the temple's layout may at first seem confusing, but there is order. The *bot* lies ahead and slightly to the right of the main entrance, in the middle of a courtyard surrounded by cloisters containing row upon row of gilded Buddha images. There are four small *viharns* on each side of the gallery, and a *chedi* and chapel stand at each of the four corners. The *bot* is most interesting for the marble bas-reliefs around its base depicting episodes from the *Ramakien*.

Other buildings of note on the left beyond the main gate are four large *chedis* (commemorating the first four Chakri Kings), numerous small *chedis*, an old manuscript

A tour of Bangkok begins with a ferry trip down the Chao Phraya river.

library, a Chinese pavilion and a European-style pavilion.

In the far left-hand corner of the compound a large chapel enshrines the temple's main attraction, a giant 46m (150ft) long statue of the Reclining Buddha. The image is made of brick covered with plaster and gold leaf. Note the soles of the feet, which are intricately inlaid in mother-of-pearl with the 108 auspicious signs of the Buddha.

Wat Phra Keo and the Grand Palace ★★★

Open daily 08:30–11:30 and 13:00–15:30. Beyond Wat Po on Sanam Chai Road are the massive white crenellated walls and huge gateways (to accommodate howdah-topped elephants) surrounding the Grand Palace and Wat Phra Keo, Temple of the Emerald Buddha. The main entrance, however, is around the corner in Na Phralan Road.

The collection of regal apartments which comprise the Grand Palace (of which only a small part is open to the public) and the royal chapel of Wat Phra Keo, the nation's holiest shrine, epitomize Bangkok sightseeing. Here is quintessential Thailand and everyone's dream of Oriental wonder.

Situated in the northeast corner of the Grand Palace compound, Wat Phra Keo was built soon after the founding of Bangkok as the capital in 1782. It comprises a group of buildings profusely adorned with gold leaf, glazed coloured tiles and mirror-glass inlay, while standing guard are statues of giant *yakshas*, golden *kinnaris* and other mythological beings.

The Grand Palace, former residence of the Thai Royal Family.

> **SACRED IMAGE**
>
> The Emerald Buddha (actually made of green jasper) is the palladium of the nation. It was reputedly first discovered in Chiang Rai in 1436, when lightning cracked a temple *chedi* to reveal the statue hidden inside. Prior to being enshrined in Wat Phra Keo on 22 March 1784, the Emerald Buddha had an eventful history, residing variously in Lampang and Chiang Rai before being taken to Laos in 1552. It remained in Vientiane until restored to Thailand by Chao Phraya Chakri, later King Rama I, in 1778.

Gilded architecture in the compound of Wat Phra Keo. The temple shelters the Emerald Buddha, Thailand's most sacred image.

Encountered in a line from the main entrance are the **Phra Sri Ratanna Chedi**, the **Phra Mondop** or library and the **Prasad Phra Thepbidon** or Royal Pantheon, containing statues of the Chakri Kings (open only once a year, on 6 April, Chakri Day). Next to the Phra Mondop is a model of Angkor Wat made at a time when Thailand held sway over much of Cambodia.

The 75cm (30in) high statue of the **Emerald Buddha**, Thailand's most sacred image, is enshrined in the sanctuary in the southern half of the compound. It has three bejewelled costumes, one for each season, which are changed at the appropriate time by the King. Smaller than most visitors expect and raised high on an ornate pedestal, the Emerald Buddha is difficult to see clearly, but the overall effect of the shrine is awesome.

The temple is surrounded by cloisters where there are mural paintings of scenes from the *Ramakien*. However, these have been restored several times and in the process have lost much of their aesthetic purity.

Note that a strict dress code is enforced – shorts and uncovered shoulders are absolutely forbidden.

While Wat Phra Keo remains the nation's prime temple, the **Grand Palace** itself is no longer the Royal Residence, though it is used for certain state functions. The oldest of the several halls date from the late 18th century; others are the product of several extensive additions made during various reigns up to the turn of the present century. Stylistic architectural variations are thus an interesting feature.

Five main buildings may be seen from the outside:

Chakri Maha Prasat, readily recognized by its Italianate façade and triple-spired Thai roof, was designed by an English architect and built during the

---

BANGKOK FACT FILE

Bangkok is by far the largest city in Thailand; the second-largest city, Chiang Mai, with a population of around 200,000, is less than 2.5% its size. One in eight Thais live in Bangkok and over 80% of the country's motor vehicles are registered there. Just over 50% of Bangkok's population is of Chinese descent, while some 70% of the country's university students study in the city.

reign of King Rama V, who took a keen interest in European art and architecture.

Dusit Maha Prasat, to the right of the Chakri Maha Prasat, was built as an audience hall by Rama I and is today used for the lying-in-state of kings. The architecture exemplifies early Ratanakosin style.

The nearby **Aphon Phimok Pavilion** is a charming little building where originally the king would alight from his palanquin and don official attire before giving an audience in the adjacent Throne Hall.

Amarin Winitchai Hall, to the left of the Chakri Maha Prasat, is one of the Palace's earliest structures, originally used as the royal court of justice and today the venue for royal birthday rites.

Furthest west is the **Boromphiman Hall**, a royal residence from the reign of King Rama VI.

Lak Muang *

On the corner of Sanam Chai and Na Phralan roads, on the opposite side from the Grand Palace, is the Lak Muang, or city shrine. This small pavilion houses the stone pillar which Rama I erected as the city's foundation stone. Home of Bangkok's guardian spirit, the shrine is deeply respected and believed a source of good fortune.

Pramane Ground

Stretching north from the Grand Palace is the oval open space of the Pramane Ground (or Sanam Luang). Traditionally the site of royal cremations, it is more generally used for public recreation and special events such as the annual Ploughing Ceremony (April), the King's birthday celebrations (December), and kite flying (February to May).

> ### LAK MUANG
>
> This pillar stands in a gracefully renovated, multi-roofed pagoda covered with gold leaf and flower garlands, and is the point from which the power of the city is said to spring; distances within the city are measured from it. Lak Muang and its attendant spirits are believed able to grant wishes, and every day scores of supplicants gather here to make offerings of flowers or press gold leaf against the monument. In an adjacent *sala* a troupe hired by successful supplicants performs Thai *lakhon* classical dance. For spectators, the best times to visit are late afternoons and holidays; supplicants should go before 11:00 as after this the spirits retire to heaven for the day.

One of many murals decorating the cloister walls of Wat Phra Keo and showing scenes from the Ramakien.

AT THE MUSEUM

Covering every period of Thai history, the National Museum in Bangkok, divided (clearly) into numerous sections, presents a number of difficult choices for visitors short of time. The best solution is to take a guided tour, departing from the entry pavilion at the main gate and lasting approximately 2hr. Alternatively, you can purchase a map and make for the halls containing your areas of chosen interest. There are English-language interpretations to help you make the most of your visit. Don't forget to look also at the museum buildings, the oldest of which date from 1782.

The National Museum houses an excellent collection of art and artefacts from all periods.

Wat Mahathat *

Open daily 09:00–17:00. Also known as the Temple of the Great Relic, the temple is situated on the west side of the Pramane Ground, between Silpakorn and Thammasat Universities. Built during the reign of Rama I, Wat Mahathat is most significant as the national headquarters of the Mahanikai monastic sect, and is renowned as the hub of Buddhist learning and as a meditation training centre.

A market is held on Buddhist holy days in and around the temple courtyard, where stalls display Buddhist texts, amulets and other religious objects, plus traditional medicines and curios.

The National Museum ***

Open Wed–Sun 09:00–16:00. The museum occupies part of a former palace, constructed in 1782, as well as several other historic buildings which provide a bonus to the exhibition halls housing an excellent collection of sculpture from all periods, ethnological exhibits and artefacts from the decorative and performing arts. Of the old buildings, the most spectacular is the **Buddhaisawan Chapel**, which contains some splendid mural paintings illustrating scenes from the life of the Buddha.

Guided tours in four different languages are provided in the mornings beginning at 09:00.

Wat Bovornivet **

Situated northeast of the Pramane Ground, on Phra Sumen Road, Wat Bovornivet is off the beaten track but worth visiting. It is distinguished as the temple where King Rama IV, prior to succeeding to the throne in 1851, founded the Thammayut monastic sect, which follows a stricter discipline than that of the older Mahanikai order. Subsequently, kings and royal princes have traditionally spent their time of monastic retreat here.

Dating mostly from the reign of King Rama III, Wat Bovornivet is also notable for its strikingly original 19th-century murals painted by Khrua In Khong, the first major Thai artist to experiment with Western stylistic influences.

Amulets for sale on a market stall. These images are widely believed to offer protection from misfortune.

LONGEST NAME

Bangkok is properly known as Krung Thep, meaning 'City of Angels', the first in a string of titles which make up the world's longest city name: Great City of Angels, the Supreme Repository of Divine Jewels, the Great Land Unconquerable, the Grand and Prominent Realm, the Royal and Delightful Capital City Full of Nine Noble Gems, the Highest Royal Dwelling and Grand Palace, the Divine Shelter and Living Place of the Reincarnated Spirits.

OLD ROYAL CITY – TOUR 2

A second tour of old Bangkok begins at the far end of Rajdamnoen Avenue, which runs eastward from the Pramane Ground. This broad boulevard was over-optimistically intended by King Rama V as Bangkok's answer to Paris's Champs Elysées. Halfway along is **Democracy Monument**, commemorating the 1932 creation of a constitutional monarchy.

Wat Rachanada **

Located on the corner of Rajdamnoen Avenue and Mahachai Road, this is one of Bangkok's most interesting and lesser-known temples. In the first courtyard is a famous amulet market, a veritable Aladdin's cave of talismans, Buddha statues and other religious objects. Beyond are the temple's *bot* and two *viharns*. The former's interior is decorated with murals depicting paradise and hell, with groups of angels in various parts of the sky. The left-hand *viharn* is notable for its unusual design and numerous Ratanakosin-style Buddha images.

Unique to Wat Rachanada is the Loha Prasat ('Metal Pavilion'), a large, multi-spired pavilion raised on a three-step pyramid behind the main temple buildings. Representing a legendary palace mentioned in the Buddhist chronicles, it is the only surviving building of its kind, similar structures in India and Sri Lanka having long since crumbled.

AMULETS

Tiny images of the Buddha, or medallions engraved with the likeness of famous monks or revered kings, along with a host of other talismanic objects such as carved wooden phalluses, are widely believed to offer protection from all manner of ills and danger. Most males (women to a lesser degree) wear at least one amulet on a gold neck-chain, while it is not uncommon to see necklaces strung with half a dozen or more. Antique or rare amulets are collectors' items and command high prices.

The Vimanmek Palace, the largest golden teak building in the world, contains a splendid assemblage of antique furniture.

Golden Mount **

On the opposite corner of Mahachai Road from Wat Rachanada are the Golden Mount and **Wat Saket**. The 78m (256ft) high artificial hill, begun in the reign of Rama III and completed in the Fifth Reign, is topped by a gilded *chedi* enshrining sacred relics of the Buddha. A circular flight of 318 steps leads up to the base of the *chedi,* from where there are fine views of the city. At the bottom of the hill is Wat Saket, built by Rama I and thus ranking among Bangkok's oldest temples.

Wat Suthat and the Giant Swing **

Open daily 09:00–17:00. Go down Mahachai Road and turn right into Bamrung Muang Road to reach Wat Suthat and the Giant Swing. Constructed in the first half of the 19th century, Wat Suthat is remarkable for its two large and impressive buildings, its superb murals and its collection of Buddha images. Among the latter is the massive **Phra Buddha Chakyamuni**, originally from Sukhothai and a masterpiece of that period's sculpture.

Opposite Wat Suthat are the red-painted 25m (82ft) twin poles of the Giant Swing, known as Sao Ching Cha, relic of a daring former Brahmanic ritual. Teams of four young men would swing until they were level with the tops of the poles. The ceremony was abolished in 1935.

Wat Rajabophit *

Another lesser-known temple, Wat Rajabophit is reached by continuing up Bamrung Muang Road, turning left into Tanao Road and then taking the first right. Constructed in 1863 by King Rama V, this attractive temple displays startling originality in design and decorative style, notably in the quasi-Gothic interiors of its two chapels and in the circular gallery surrounding the *chedi*.

DUSIT

Lying to the north of old royal Bangkok, the spacious, tree-lined avenues of the Dusit area present a striking contrast, and give the area an almost European feel. It was first groomed as the city's 'new' royal quarter at the turn of the 20th century by King Rama V, a monarch renowned for his progressive policies and interest in the West. Although the present royal residence, **Chitralada Palace**, is located in Dusit, its extensive grounds effectively hide it from public gaze.

Vimanmek Palace **

Open daily 09:30–16:00. Billed as the world's largest mansion built of golden teak, Vimanmek Palace is located behind Bangkok's **National Assembly** at the end of Rachadamnoen Nok Avenue. Originally a home of King Rama V, this splendid three-storey, 81-room mansion is an architectural gem. Inside is a collection of furniture, ceramics and other artefacts from the Fifth Reign.

Dusit Zoo *

Open daily 08:00–18:00. Next to the National Assembly near Vimanmek Palace, Dusit Zoo provides one of Bangkok's few quiet, green areas, although the collection of animals is unremarkable. Also in the grounds is a lake where pedaloes and rowing boats can be hired.

Wat Benchamabophit, The Marble Temple **

Open daily 07:00–17:00. This is the supreme example of Thai religious architecture in the modern period. Located on Sri Ayutthaya Road, the temple is famous for its royal *bot*, completed in 1900 on the orders of King Rama V. Faced with white Carrara marble, the building displays surprising unity and symmetry.

The imposing Buddha image inside the *bot* is a copy of the famous Jinaraja (Chinaraj) statue of Phitsanulok. In the courtyard behind the temple is a collection of more than 50 Buddha images, some originals, some copies, illustrating sculpture styles from various periods and diverse locales.

Inside the Vimanmek Palace.

Multicoloured Chinese porcelain decorates the terraces of Wat Arun, the 'Temple of the Dawn'.

THONBURI TEMPLES

In spite of a brief spell as Thailand's capital in the 18th century, Thonburi, on the west bank of the Chao Phraya, today shows little evidence of its past and is largely suburban in character. It does, however, boast a few noteworthy temples.

Wat Arun, Temple of the Dawn **

Open daily 08:30–17:30. Most famous of the Thonburi temples, Wat Arun is a Bangkok landmark with its 79m (259ft) high *prang*. This finger-like spire is raised on a series of terraces and is decorated with embedded pieces of multicoloured porcelain. A staircase and balconies wind their way around the outside of the tower, affording panoramic views. The temple catches the rays of the early morning sun, hence the popular name, although the building is seen to best effect from the Bangkok side of the river at sunset.

Wat Kalayanimit *

A little way downstream from Wat Arun, Wat Kalayanimit stands out because of its unusually tall sanctuary. The temple compound and monks' quarters are substantially unchanged and this, combined with the riverside setting, produces one of the few spots in the city where it is possible to picture the Bangkok of old.

Wat Prayoon *

A short distance below Wat Kalayanimit, this temple is intriguing for the artificial hill in the compound, dotted with small *chedis* and frangipani trees, and surrounded by a pool filled with turtles. It was reportedly designed by King Rama III, who one night became fascinated by the shape of the mound of molten wax from his candle.

KLONG TOUR

Most of Bangkok's few surviving canals (*klongs*) are in Thonburi. Touring these by longtail boat reveals a slice of traditional riverine life. Longtail boats (typical river transport so-called on account of their long propeller shafts) can be hired from the various landing stages along the Chao Phraya, one of the most convenient being next to the Oriental Hotel (Tha Orienten). Prices are negotiable.

CHINATOWN

When Bangkok was chosen as Thailand's capital, the Chinese traders occupying the river bank were moved back to make space for the Grand Palace and other buildings. They were resettled southeast of the old royal city in a district which today remains Chinatown, centred on Charoen Krung and Yaowaraj roads.

Characterized by crowded narrow streets packed with small shops selling herbal medicines and other ethnic products, Chinatown is a delight for inveterate browsers. Most typical of the district is **Sampeng Lane** (Soi Wanit), which is jammed with a heady mix of exotic goods.

At Sampeng Lane's western end is **Pahurat**, where the ethnic flavour changes to Indian and the main merchandise is cloth.

A little to the north, between Yaowaraj and Charoen Krung roads, is **Nakhon Kasem** (Thieves' Market), no longer selling hot goods but offering a curious mix of old and new, especially brassware, chests, cabinets and other furniture.

Bangkok's Chinatown is a browser's paradise of ethnic shops.

Wat Traimit **

Open daily 09:00–17:00. On the southeast edge of Chinatown, between Yaowaraj and Charoen Krung roads, Wat Traimit ('Temple of the Golden Buddha') is famous for its 3m (10ft) high solid gold statue of the Buddha, weighing 5.5 tonnes. The image is a fine example of the Sukhothai style of Thai sculpture.

THAI HOUSES

In the past when Thais moved house, they did literally that, taking their home to pieces and carting it to a new location. Made of teak and raised on wooden stilts as protection from floods and wild animals, traditional Thai houses are prefabricated structures made up of movable panels attached to sturdy columns and beams by wooden pegs; no nails are used in the construction.

GOOD LUCK

The Erawan Shrine on the corner of Ploenchit and Rajdamri Road is Bangkok's most famous source of good fortune. This ornate shrine to the Hindu god Brahma was erected in the 1950s during the construction of the adjoining Erawan Hotel (today replaced by the Grand Hyatt Erawan). The project was plagued by mishaps which abruptly ceased after a Brahman priest suggested the shrine. Supplicants flock daily to the shrine to ask for good fortune and make offerings.

FLOATING MARKETS

There are two floating markets, where fruit, vegetables and other goods are sold from small sampans. The one in **Thonburi** is grossly over-commercialized and should be avoided. Further afield, the **Damnoen Saduak** floating market is more authentic but still rather touristy. Regular early-morning tours are operated daily by leading travel agents.

SECULAR SIGHTS

Jim Thompson's House ★★

Open Mon–Sat 09:00–17:00. The former home of Jim Thompson, the man who revitalized the Thai silk industry after World War II, is located at Soi Kasemsan 2, off Rama I Road opposite the National Stadium. In 1967 he disappeared in the Cameron Highlands of Malaysia under mysterious circumstances. Now preserved as a private museum, the Thompson house is an excellent example of traditional Thai domestic architecture, while inside is displayed Thompson's impressive collection of Oriental antiques.

Suan Pakkard Palace ★★

Open daily except Sundays, 09:00–16:00. The former residence of the late Princess Chumbhot of Nagara Svarga on Si Ayutthaya Road has five traditional Thai houses overlooking a landscaped garden. The houses contain a collection of Asian antiques, while the highlight is a 300-year-old lacquer pavilion, its interior walls displaying the Thai decorative art of gilt on black lacquer.

Jim Thompson's house, now a private museum, was once the home of the legendary silk entrepreneur.

Sampans in the floating market at Damnoen Saduak.

Two of the best trips are to **Ayutthaya** and to the **River Kwai** (taking in **Nakhon Pathom** on the way); both are described in detail in Chapter 3.

• **Ancient City**: Occupying a 80ha (200-acre) site some 33km (20 miles) from Bangkok on the Sukhumvit Highway in Samut Prakan province, the Ancient City is an open-air museum displaying 89 scaled-down replicas of Thailand's most famous historical monuments. Open daily 08:30–17:30.

• **Samphran Elephant Ground and Zoo**: 30km (19 miles) west of Bangkok, this is a good place to take children. Plenty of animals as well as crocodile wrestling, performing elephants and a magic show. Open daily 08:30–18:00.

• **Rose Garden Country Resort**: A short distance beyond Samphran Elephant Ground and Zoo, this features landscaped gardens and a golf course, though the most popular attraction is its Thai Cultural Village with shows of folk dancing, Thai boxing and sword fighting every afternoon at 15:00. Open daily 08:00–18:00.

• **Safari World**: A variety of wild animals including zebras, deer, giraffes, tigers, lions and birds in a parkland setting, with the additional attraction of a marine park. Open daily 09:00–18:00.

Snake Farm *

Open weekdays 08:30–15:30, weekends and public holidays 08:30–11:00. On Rama IV Road near Lumpini Park, the **Pasteur Institute**, part of the Thai Red Cross, is famous for its large collection of poisonous snakes from whose venom snake-bite sera are made. Demonstrations of snake handling and venom extraction are given at 10:30 and 14:00, and these are undoubtedly the best times to visit.

Weekend Market **

Sat–Sun 06:00–18:00. In the northern part of the city at Chatuchak Park, off Phaholyothin Road near the Northern Bus Terminal, this open-air market is a browser's paradise, jammed with hundreds of stalls selling just about everything from potted plants to practically new antiques, from cassettes to clothing, from socks to souvenirs.

Bangkok at a Glance

GETTING THERE

Bangkok International Airport is at Don Muang some 25km (15 miles) from the city. Traffic is nearly always heavy and the drive can take 45min-2hr. Limousine service counters in the Arrival Hall offer car or minibus trips into town, though ordinary taxis are slightly cheaper (counter next to Arrival Hall exit). A special airport train service is more economical (take walkway to Airport Hotel to reach station platform). Ordinary buses stop outside the airport but are not recommended for first-time arrivals burdened with luggage. Ignore touts in the Arrival Hall offering hotels, tours, etc. If you expect to be met by a travel agent representative, make sure of his/her ID.

GETTING AROUND

Car hire: Drivers must be over 21 and have an international licence. Car hire agencies in Bangkok: Avis, tel 255–5300; Bangkok Car Rent, tel 252–6428: Chao Phraya Car Rent, tel 258–2651; Hertz, tel 251–7575.

Taxis: The most comfortable transport option. Nearly all are metered and air-conditioned. No tipping expected.

Tuk Tuks: A Bangkok specialty, correctly called *samlors* (literally 'three wheels'). Noisy, unstable and open to traffic fumes but cheaper than ordinary taxis. Fares are negotiable and must be agreed

before embarking on journey. **Motorbike taxis**: Quickest if not safest way to get through Bangkok traffic. Riders wear numbered vests and taxi ranks are typically found at the entrance to the longer *sois* (lanes).

Buses: Ordinary buses are slightly cheaper than the air-conditioned ones; fares vary depending on distance.

River taxis: Cross-river taxis are cheap. Other boats criss-cross the river calling at landing stages on both banks.

WHERE TO STAY

Bangkok offers an enormous choice of accommodation in all categories from 'Best in the World' to cheap guesthouses.

Silom Area and Riverside
Dusit Thani, 946 Rama IV Road, tel 236–0450, fax 236–6400
Central location at end of Silom Road opposite Lumpini Park.

Oriental, 48 Oriental Avenue, off New Road, tel 236–0400, fax 236–1939
Where the rich and famous stay.

Shangri-La, 89 Soi Wat Suan Plu, off New Road, tel 236–7777, fax 236–8570
Arguably the best river frontage of all hotels on the Chao Phraya.

The Sukhothai, 13/3 South Sathorn Road, tel 287–0222, fax 287–4980
Interior design is a brilliant modern interpretation of classical Thai style.

Rajdamri/Ploenchit/Rama I Area
Grand Hyatt Erawan, 494 Rajdamri Road, tel 254–1234, fax 253–5856
Central location next to Erawan Shrine.

Hilton International, Nai Lert Park, 2 Wireless Road, tel 253–0123, fax 253–6509
Extensive landscaped tropical gardens.

Regent Bangkok, 155 Rajdamri Road, tel 251–6127, fax 253–9195
As central a location as you'll find in Bangkok; great lobby for city rendezvous.

Siam Intercontinental, 967 Rama I Road, tel 253–0355, fax 253–2275
Large park-like garden ensures quiet in a fairly central location.

Sukhumvit
Landmark, 138 Sukhumvit Road, tel 254–0404, fax 253–4259
Fine facilities and good location.

Federal, 27 Soi 11, Sukhumvit Road, tel 253–0175, fax 253–5332
Originally built as an R&R hotel for US servicemen during Vietnam War; good value.

Impala, 9 Soi 24, Sukhumvit Road, tel 258–8612, fax 259–2896
Good facilities in the heart of the Sukhumvit area.

Jim's Lodge, 125/7 Soi Ruamrudee, tel 255–3100, fax 253–8492
Very comfortable and excel-

Bangkok at a Glance

lent value; situated between the Sukhumvit and Silom areas.

Mermaid's Rest, Soi 8, Sukhumvit Road, tel 253–3648

Small but comfortable with garden setting and good food.

WHERE TO EAT

As with hotels, Bangkok boasts an extraordinary number and variety of restaurants in all categories. Your best bet is to look for restaurants obviously popular with the locals, or consult the classified section of the *Bangkok Post*.

Silom/New Road

Bussaracum, 35 Soi Pipat 2, off Convent Road, tel 235–8915

Expensive but very good authentic Thai food.

China House, Oriental Hotel, 48 Oriental Avenue (off New Road), tel 236–0400

Superb Cantonese food and plenty of atmosphere in old house adjacent to hotel.

Himali Cha Cha, 1229/11 New Road, tel 235–1569

North Indian cuisine and vegetarian dishes at moderate prices.

Sawasdee, Soi Pipat (off Sathorn), tel 237–6310

Thai food with classical dance show.

Sukhumvit

Cabbages and Condoms, Sukhumvit Soi 12, tel 252–5160

Good and reasonably priced

Thai food; run by the Population and Community Development Association (hence the name).

Lemon Grass, Sukhumvit Soi 24, tel 258–8637

Thai version of nouvelle cuisine in traditional house setting.

Wireless Road/Ruamrudee

Ma Maison, Hilton International, Nai Lert Park, 2 Wireless Road, tel 253–0123

Superb European food and impeccable service in elegant Thai setting.

Neil's Tavern, 58/4 Soi Ruamrudee, tel 251–5644

Good steaks and seafood in a pleasant atmosphere.

SHOPPING

Shopping in Bangkok is excellent, offering quality buys as well as a host of handicrafts and souvenirs. Most famous of the deluxe items is Thai silk, sold either by the yard or as made-up items. **Jim Thompson's Thai Silk Factory** on Suriwong Road has the best-known – and generally most expensive – products, but there are several other establishments around town. Known for its silk fashions is **Khanitha**, also on

Suriwong Road, while tailormade clothing in general is a Bangkok speciality. The other top-quality buys are gems and jewellery (Bangkok is a world centre for coloured gemstones) and Thai, Burmese, Khmer and Chinese antiques. Jewellery stores are found in all shopping areas, while best for antiques is **River City Shopping Complex** (off New Road next to the Royal Orchid Sheraton hotel), where the entire fourth floor is devoted to antique shops. The Tourist Authority of Thailand (TAT) has a list of approved shops and can also handle customer complaints. Handicrafts and folk art products (ideal interior decor items) include bronzeware, ceramics, woodcarving and silverware.

TOURS AND EXCURSIONS

Numerous tour operators offer a host of city sightseeing tours and upcountry trips covering all parts of Thailand. Try: **Diethelm Travel**, Kian Gwan Building II, 140/1 Wireless Rd, tel 255–9150, fax 256–0248. **East West (Travel) Group**, 135 Soi Polo, Wireless Road, tel 253–0681, fax 253–6178. **World Travel Service**, 1053 New Road, tel 233–5900.

BANGKOK	J	F	M	A	M	J	J	A	S	O	N	D
AVERAGE TEMP. °F	79	81	84	86	85	84	83	82	82	32	80	78
AVERAGE TEMP. °C	26	27	29	30	29	29	28	28	28	27	27	26
Hours of Sun Daily	9	8	9	8	7	6	6	6	5	6	7	8
RAINFALL in	1	1	1	1	9	7	8	8	14	10	2	1
RAINFALL mm	9	30	29	35	220	149	154	197	344	242	48	10
Days of Rainfall	1	3	3	6	16	16	19	20	21	17	6	1

3
Central Thailand

Extending north and west from Bangkok, the Central Plains is an immensely fertile region characterized by a patchwork of rice paddies dotted with sizeable towns. It is bounded in the west by the saw-tooth mountains which form the border with Burma, and in the east by the **Khorat plateau**. In the north, the town of **Tak** marks approximately the end of the plains and the beginning of the northern uplands. Flowing north–south through the entire area is the **Chao Phraya river system**, which accounts for the region's fertility.

The nation's agricultural heartland is also its historical heart. **Nakhon Pathom**, west of Bangkok, was a Mon power centre in ancient times, while beyond lies **Kanchanaburi**, site of the infamous World War II Bridge over the River Kwai, and **Three Pagodas Pass**, a former gateway for Burmese invaders.

North of Bangkok are the ruins of **Ayutthaya**, Thailand's capital for more than 400 years and once the most magnificent city in the Orient. Beyond lies the historic town of **Lop Buri**, a Khmer outpost before the rise of the Thais and later serving as Versailles to Ayutthaya's Paris.

On the upper edge of the Central Plains is the 700-year-old site of **Sukhothai**, Thailand's first capital. Nearby are the ruins of the ancient satellite towns **Si Satchanalai** and **Kamphaeng Phet**. To the west, a road crosses spectacular mountain scenery to reach **Mae Sot** on the Burmese borders.

For touring purposes, the Central Plains can be

CLIMATE

The Central Plains have essentially the same climate as Bangkok. However, note that Sukhothai occupies a sort of topographical bowl which can trap the heat, making touring the site uncomfortable in the hot season when the mercury can hit 40°C (104°F).

Opposite: *Wat Sra Sri is among the twenty major shrines in Sukhothai Historical Park.*

DON'T MISS

*** **Ayutthaya**: Thailand's former capital spanning four centuries.
** **Lop Buri**: Ancient city with monuments to an illustrious past.
*** **Sukhothai Historical Park**: Site of the birth of the nation.
** **Nakhon Pathom**: World's tallest Buddhist monument.
** **Kanchanaburi**: Bridge over River Kwai and beautiful natural scenery.

included on a road or rail route north to Chiang Mai, although Ayutthaya is also a popular day excursion from Bangkok. Kanchanaburi lies off the north–south axis and warrants a separate visit.

NAKHON PATHOM

The town of Nakhon Pathom ('First City'), situated on Highway 4 some 56km (35 miles) west of Bangkok, occupies the site of one of the region's earliest settlements, rising to prominence as the capital of a Mon kingdom during the Dvaravati period (6th–11th centuries). A couple of hours' sightseeing is sufficient, either on a day trip from Bangkok or on the way to Kanchanaburi.

Phra Pathom Chedi **

In the heart of town, this ranks as the world's tallest Buddhist monument at 120m (393ft) high. It is also one of Thailand's most important places of worship, as reputedly the site where Buddhism first took root on what is now Thai soil. The original Mon-period *chedi* was badly damaged by the Burmese in 1057 and the huge bell-shaped monument seen today dates from the 19th century. The impressive building is raised on a series of terraces and surrounded by cloisters with chapels at the four cardinal points.

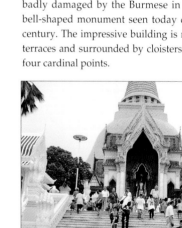

The towering landmark of Phra Pathom Chedi, tallest Buddhist monument in the world.

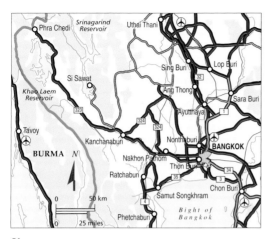

KANCHANABURI

The site of the **Bridge over the River Kwai** lies 130km (80 miles) west of Bangkok and is also the administrative centre of Kanchanaburi province, noted for its extraordinary scenic beauty. The town stands at the junction of the Kwai Noi and Kwai Yai, twin rivers which join to form the Mae Klong. Upstream, the wooded valleys of both the Kwai Noi and Kwai Yai are liberally scattered with caves, waterfalls and scenic spots. The town and the bridge can be seen on a day trip from Bangkok, but Kanchanaburi's bigger draws are its river resort hotels and river rafts which offer the best way to appreciate exceptionally lovely natural settings.

Major Sights

• **War cemeteries**: Kanchanaburi War Cemetery on Saeng Chuto Road contains the remains of 6982 PoWs who died during the construction of the Death Railway. A further 1750 graves are at the Chong-kai Cemetery, on the opposite bank of the river southwest of town.

• **JEATH War Museum**: On Pak Phraek Road near the entrance to Wat Chumphon, this small museum, a reconstruction of a PoW camp, poignantly documents the horrors endured by the prisoners. Open daily 08:30–16:30.

• **Wat Tham Mangkhon Thong**: Approximately 4km

DEATH RAILWAY

During World War II, the Japanese wanted a rail supply link between Thailand and Burma. Engineers estimated it would take five years to build the 415km (258-mile) railway – the Japanese army had it completed in 16 months at the cost of the lives of 16,000 PoWs and an estimated 100,000 civilian forced labourers who died from inhumane treatment, malnutrition and disease. After the war the Thai section between Nam Tok and Three Pagodas Pass was dismantled.

*The infamous Bridge over
the River Kwai, partially
rebuilt after World War II,
is still in use.*

**BRIDGE OVER THE
RIVER KWAI**

On the northern edge of the
town, the bridge spanning
the Kwai Yai river is smaller
and less impressive than it
appears in David Lean's film.
It was bombed in 1945 but
the curved spans are original
sections. The bridge is still in
use and the 2hr train ride to
the end of the line at Nam
Tok is especially scenic.

THREE PAGODAS PASS

Situated some 200km (125
miles) from Kanchanaburi
town, the bell-shaped *chedis*
from which this spot on the
Thai–Burmese border derives
its name are visually insignifi-
cant, but the mountain
scenery is breathtaking. To
get there, take a bus from
Kanchanaburi town to
Sangkhlaburi (an atmospheric
little outpost inhabited mainly
by Mon, Karen and Burmese
and with an interesting
morning market) then
minibus to Three Pagodas.
Travellers without their own
transport will need to
overnight in Sangkhlaburi.

(2¹/₂ miles) southwest of town, the 'Cave Temple of the
Golden Dragon', once famous for a nun who meditated
floating on her back in a pool, is worth visiting for its hilltop cave temple reached via a long, steep flight of steps.
• **Ban Keo Neolithic Museum**: This small museum
35km (21 miles) west of Kanchanaburi town contains
Neolithic remains and utensils first unearthed at the site
by a Dutch PoW working on the Death Railway. Open
Wed–Sun 09:00–16:00.
• **Prasat Muang Singh**: Some 10km (6 miles) beyond Ban
Keo are the ruins of a 13th-century Khmer temple complex constructed out of huge laterite blocks. The site is
impressive in extent but architecturally disappointing.
Open daily 08:00–16:00.
• **Erawan National Park**: Located in the valley of the
Kwai Yai 72km (45 miles) to the north, this attractive
slice of countryside is accessible by forest trail and has a
series of small waterfalls as its focal point. Buses for the
90min journey to the park depart from Kanchanaburi
town every 50min 08:00–16:00.
• **Sai Yok Noi and Sai Yok Yai Waterfalls**: Set in the
Kwai Noi valley, these waterfalls are more impressive
than those at Erawan. Sai Yok Noi lies just beyond Nam
Tok railway station, about 77km (48 miles) northwest of
Kanchanaburi town. Sai Yok Yai has the added attraction
of **Kaeng Lawa Cave** and can be reached by boat, a
2¹/₂hr journey upstream from Pak-Saeng Pier.

Ayutthaya

Thailand's capital from 1350 to 1767, Ayutthaya is the nation's best-known historical site. Burmese invaders made a thorough job of sacking the original city and the surviving ruins are scattered around an uninspiring modern provincial centre 80km (50 miles) north of Bangkok.

Major Monuments

• **Wat Phra Sri Sanphet**: The royal temple within the compound of the now vanished king's palace, originally built in 1448 and restored at least twice. One of Ayutthaya's most famous ruins, it is distinguished by a row of three finely restored Ayutthaya-style *chedis*.

• **Viharn Phra Mongkol Bopit**: Close to Wat Phra Sri Sanphet, this modern building enshrines one of the largest bronze Buddha images in Thailand.

• **Wat Phra Ram**: Southeast of Wat Phra Sri Sanphet, this temple is easily identified by its large central *prang*. It was built in 1369 by King Ramesuen, Ayutthaya's second king, on the cremation site of his father, King U Thong.

• **Wat Mahathat**: Across the lake east of Wat Phra Ram, this was once an extensive temple complex first built in 1374, although now it is in ruins. The impressive *prang* seen today was originally twice its present height.

• **Wat Rachaburana**: Directly north of Wat Mahathat, this fine temple, in a comparatively good state of preser-

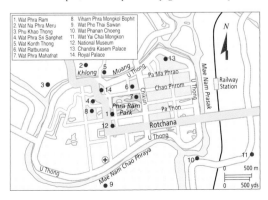

1. Wat Phra Ram
2. Wat Na Phra Meru
3. Phu Khao Thong
4. Wat Phra Sri Sanphet
5. Wat Konth Thong
6. Wat Ratburana
7. Wat Phra Mahathat
8. Viharn Phra Mongkol Bophit
9. Wat Pho Thai Sawan
10. Wat Phanan Choeng
11. Wat Yai Chai Mongkon
12. National Museum
13. Chandra Kasem Palace
14. Royal Palace

> ### ISLAND CITY
>
> At the confluence of the Lop Buri, Pasak and Chao Phraya rivers, Ayutthaya was created as an island city. It was surrounded by a 12km (7½-mile) fortified wall and crisscrossed by a 140km (88-mile) network of canals. At the 17th-century height of its power it had an estimated population of one million, three major palace complexes and some 400 temples. Many of the buildings were lavishly decorated with gold. Portuguese, Dutch, French, British and Japanese trade factories made it a truly cosmopolitan city.

AYUTTHAYA MUSEUMS

Ayutthaya has three muse-
ums: **Chao Sam Phraya
National Museum**
(Wed–Sun 09:00–16:00) contains the most important
Ayutthaya finds; **Historical
Study Centre** (Mon–Fri
09:30–15:30, Sat–Sun
09:30–16:30) is a modern
museum with reconstructions
and other educational
exhibits; **Chandra Kasem
Palace** (Wed–Sun
09:00–12:00, 13:00–16:00) is
a historic building recon-
structed in the 19th century
by King Rama IV.

vation, was built in 1424 by King Borommaracha II on
the cremation site of his two elder brothers, who killed
each other in a struggle for the throne. The crypt of the
prang was excavated in 1957, revealing traces of mural
paintings and a collection of gold objects and jewellery
now in the Chao Sam Phraya National Museum.

• **Wat Na Phra Mane**: Opposite the royal palace on the
north side of the Lop Buri river, this is Ayutthaya's best-
preserved temple. The *bot* is a good example of early
Ayutthaya architectural style and enshrines a 6m (19ft)
bronze Buddha image in royal attire, typical of late
Ayutthaya sculpture. Of note in the *viharn* is a Dvaravati
stone Buddha image seated in 'European' fashion with
hands on knees.

• **Wat Yai Chai Mongkol**: Across the Pasak river in a
southeasterly direction, this temple was originally built
in 1357 but is most distinguished for its *chedi*, constructed to commemorate King Naresuan's victory in single-
handed combat on elephant-back over the Crown Prince
of Burma in 1592.

• **Wat Phanan Choeng**: West of Wat Yai Chai Mongkol,
close to the river bank, the temple is believed to predate
the founding of Ayutthaya by some 26 years, since its

*Ruined temple complex at
Ayutthaya, Thailand's
most famous historical site.*

Water pavilion in the grounds of the Royal Summer Palace at Bang Pa-In.

> **ROYAL TRAGEDY**
>
> A monument in the grounds of Bang Pa-In commemorates the death in 1881 of Queen Sunanda, a favourite wife of King Rama V, who drowned in the river when her boat capsized. Although she could have been rescued, the boatmen were powerless to help as a Palace Law prohibited them from touching royalty. If they had attempted to take hold of the Queen they would have faced execution.

revered 19m (62ft) image of the seated Buddha dates from 1324.

• **Phu Khao Thong**: On open ground 2km (1¹/₄ miles) northwest of the city, this monument rises imposingly above the flat countryside. The *chedi* was originally built by the Burmese in 1569 to mark their first conquest of Ayutthaya, but the present structure dates from 1745.

Bang Pa-In *

Open daily 08:30–15:30. On the banks of the Chao Phraya river 20km (12¹/₂ miles) downstream from Ayutthaya is the royal summer palace of Bang Pa-In. Although the site dates back to the Ayutthaya period, the present buildings were constructed in the late 19th and early 20th centuries. The complex is attractively laid-out and displays a

> **BEST CRUISE**
>
> Of several river cruises from Bangkok to Bang Pa-In and Ayutthaya the best is by the Mekhala, a luxuriously converted traditional wooden rice barge. The two-day trip (one way by minibus) reveals more of traditional Thailand than a week of conventional sightseeing. Contact Siam Exclusive Tours in Bangkok, tel 256–7144.

surprising variety of architectural styles, including Thai, Chinese, Italian and Victorian. Bang Pa-In is included on virtually all organized tours to Ayutthaya; alternatively, it can be reached by minibus from town.

Lop Buri

Present-day Lop Buri, 155km (96 miles) north of Bangkok on the river of the same name, is an unattractive provincial capital masking a distinguished history. A half-day's sightseeing yields a fascinating insight into Thailand's past.

With roots stretching back into prehistory, Lop Buri was a major centre of the Dvaravati Kingdom between the 7th and 11th centuries. During the 10th to late 13th centuries it became a Khmer outpost. Historical importance peaked in the 17th century when King Narai (reigned 1656–88) made the city his second capital (after Ayutthaya). It was at Lop Buri, originally called Louvo, that much of the drama of Narai's final years was played out as he and his first minister Phaulkon courted the French, only to be defeated by a palace revolution in 1688.

Lop Buri in central Thailand still retains strong cultural traditions. Here, dancers in spectacular headdresses and golden anklets perform a traditional folk dance.

Major Monuments

• **Wat Phra Si Ratana Mahathat:** Although the origins of this extensive temple ruin are unknown, construction clearly spans the Khmer period and King Narai's reign. The site is dominated by a large laterite *prang*, probably erected in the 12th century and remodelled in the 14th. Also of note is the large brick *viharn*, dating from Narai's reign and showing Western and Persian influences in its pointed-arch windows. Open daily 08:00–16:30.

• **Phra Narai Rajaivet**: Surrounded by high crenellated walls, King Narai's Palace was built between 1665 and 1677. Much of it is now in ruins but what does survive is well maintained. Partially designed by French architects, the palace was divided into three compounds enclosing, respectively, government offices, ceremonial buildings and Narai's private apartments. In the first compound are the remains of storehouses, a reservoir and what were once stables for the King's elephants. In an adjacent quadrangle are the ruins of the reception hall and the Phra Chao Hao building, which may once have enshrined an important Buddha image. Ruins in the heart of the palace include traces of the Suttha Sawan Pavilion, where Narai died, and the Dusit Sawan Thanya Maha Prasat, formerly used for receiving foreign ambassadors. Also in this inner courtyard is a 19th-century pavilion, constructed by King Rama IV and now a museum housing a good collection of Lop Buri-style sculpture and other artefacts. Open Wed–Sun 09:00–12:00, 13:00–16:00.

• **Wat Sao Tong Thong**: North of the palace close to the river, the temple's *viharn* was a Christian chapel during Narai's reign and displays a mix of Thai and quasi-Gothic styles typical of the period.

• **Ban Wichayen (Phaulkon's House)**: The house built by Narai's first minister, the Greek adventurer Phaulkon (given the Thai title Chao Phraya Wichayen), stands across the street from Wat Sao Tong Thong. Within the walled compound can be seen the ruins of Phaulkon's house, a Catholic church and Jesuit residence, and the accommodation provided for members of the 1685

GOLDEN AGE

The name 'Sukhothai' translates as 'Dawn of Happiness'
and the period is regarded as
Thailand's golden age, an
almost Utopian era. Such a
view is based on a stone
inscription attributed to
Sukhothai's most important
monarch, King Ramkam-
haeng (reigned c1279–98),
although its authenticity is
doubted by some historians.
A replica of the inscription
can be found in the
Ramkamhaeng National
Museum, and reads in part:
'In the water there are fish, in
the fields there is rice. The
ruler does not levy a tax . . .
Whoever wants to trade in
elephants, so trades.
Whoever wants to trade in
horses, so trades . . .'

French embassy. The architecture is fascinating for its
obvious European borrowings juxtaposed with Thai
forms. Open daily 08:00–16:30.

• **Phra Prang Sam Yot**: Next to the railway crossing, this
was originally a Hindu shrine and later converted to
Buddhist use. Dating from the 13th century, it comprises
three *prangs* linked by a central corridor.

SUKHOTHAI

Thailand's first capital, Sukhothai lies on the northern
edge of the Central Plains, 425km (265 miles) north of
Bangkok and 350km (215 miles) south of Chiang Mai.
Caught midway between these two major destinations,
Sukhothai falls into a touring black hole, which is unfor-
tunate as Thailand's foremost historical site should not
be missed. Moreover, this area of the upper plains
includes other destinations of not inconsiderable interest
– the ancient Sukhothai satellite towns of Si Satchanalai
and Kamphaeng Phet, as well as Phitsanulok, Tak and
Mae Sot.

Sukhothai Historical Park

Open daily 08:30–16:30. The ancient site is situated 12km
(7¹/₂ miles) west of the new town of Sukhothai.
Following the completion of a 10-year UNESCO restoration project, it is now a manicured historical park covering a total area of 70 sq km (27 sq miles), with lawns and

WHEN TO VISIT

The best time to visit
Sukhothai is during the full
moon of the 12th lunar
month – normally mid-Nov –
when Thailand's most
enchanting festival, **Loy
Krathong**, is held. The festival, believed to have originat-
ed over 700 years ago, pays
homage to Mae Khongkha,
goddess of rivers and waterways. Today, thousands of
people gather by the lake to
launch little lotus-shaped
boats (*krathongs*) bearing
offerings of flowers, candles
and incense, and to enjoy
colourful processions and a
fireworks display.

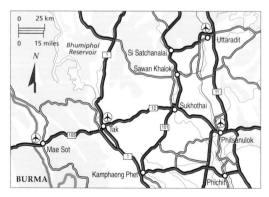

ornamental ponds set against a distant background of wooded hills. Within the confines of the ancient city's ramparts are more than 20 major monuments, while numerous other sights are scattered throughout the park.

The best starting point for a tour of the site is the **Ramkamhaeng National Museum** (Wed–Sun 09:00–16:00), which provides a useful introduction to the period. The museum is next to the core of old Sukhothai, whose principal monuments within the city walls are described below.

• **Wat Mahathat**: The biggest and most magnificent of Sukhothai's temples, dominated by a *chedi* in the form of a lotus bud. On the surrounding platform are four *stupas* and four *prangs*, while the base is decorated with stucco figures of Buddhist disciples. To the sides are two giant statues of the standing Buddha, and on the eastern side are twin rows of pillars and a platform with a large image of the seated Buddha.

• **Wat Sri Sawai**: Southwest of Wat Mahathat, this temple is distinguished by three large Khmer-style *prangs*. It possibly predates the founding of the Thai capital and was probably first built as a shrine to the Hindu god Siva before being converted to Buddhist use.

• **Wat Trapang Ngoen**: West of Wat Mahathat, the temple is picturesquely sited on an island in the middle of an ornamental lake.

• **Wat Sra Sri**: Another island temple, north of Wat

SUKHOTHAI ART

Sukhothai marks the first and perhaps finest flowering of Thai sculpture. Typically, Sukhothai Buddha images are highly stylized and are marked by fluidity of line and an uncanny degree of serenity and spirituality expressed in the facial features. Unique is the image of the walking Buddha, sculpted in the round for the first time by Sukhothai artists.

Frieze of Buddhist monks surrounding the base of a platform at Wat Mahathat, Sukhothai.

Mahathat, noted for its fine Sri Lankan-style *chedi* and the remains of a large *viharn* with a stucco Buddha image.

Of the several monuments outside the old city walls, two are essential:

• **Wat Phra Phai Luang**: A 10min walk beyond the northern gateway is an extensive ruin that rivals Wat Mahathat in importance. Its Khmer-style *prang* (the only one remaining of the original three) predates the Thai period. In front of the *prang* are the ruins of a *viharn* and a *chedi*, the base of the latter being decorated with stucco Buddha images. Nearby is a *mondop* enclosing the ruined statues of the Buddha in walking, standing, sitting and reclining postures.

• **Wat Si Chum**: Southwest of Wat Phra Phai Luang, the temple is impressive for its huge *mondop* built around an enormous stucco-over-brick statue of the seated Buddha, measuring 11.3m (37ft) across the lap. Inside the walls of the *mondop* is a narrow passage whose ceiling is decorated with beautifully engraved slabs illustrating scenes from the *Jataka* tales.

At Wat Chang Lom, in Si Satchanalai, elephant buttresses support the base of the large chedi.

PHITSANULOK AND SURROUNDS

Pleasantly sited on the banks of the Nan river 55km (35 miles) southeast of Sukhothai, Phitsanulok makes a good base for exploring the area. Sightseeing includes the large and fascinating temple complex of Wat Phra Sri Ratana Mahathat, famous for the revered Buddha image of Phra Buddha Chinaraj (Jinaraja).

Si Satchanalai ★★★

On the west bank of the Yom river 56km (35 miles) to the north of Sukhothai, Si Satchanalai was a contemporary satellite city of Sukhothai and today is similarly preserved as a historical park (open daily 08:30–16:30). Compact and attractively sited, the ruins are less visited and more atmospheric than those of Sukhothai. Dominating the site is **Wat Chang Lom**, a late-13th-century temple with a large bell-shaped *chedi* raised on a square base decorated with elephant buttresses. To the north, two temple-topped hills afford splendid panoramic views.

About 2km (1 mile) east of Si Satchanalai on the

A houseboat restaurant on the Nan river at Phitsanulok.

POTTERY CENTRE

The area around Si Satchanalai was renowned for its distinctive Sawankhalok pottery, a major export item during the Sukhothai and Ayutthaya eras. More than 200 kilns have been identified in the Si Satchanalai area and an excavated production site is on view, along with a ceramics display, at the 'Centre for the Study and Preservation of Sawankhalok Kilns' at Ban Khao Noi north of Si Satchanalai Historical Park.

Market scene at Mae Sot.

banks of the Yom river is the ancient site of Chalieng incorporating the extensive remains of Wat Si Ratana Mahathat, arguably the single most evocative temple ruin in the entire Sukhothai region. Note the superb laterite and stucco high-relief of the walking Buddha on the side of the ruined sanctuary adjoining the *prang*.

Kamphaeng Phet *

Located 77km (48 miles) south of Sukhothai, just off Highway 1, Kamphaeng Phet was another satellite town of Sukhothai. It is dotted with ruins, although they are inferior to those of Si Satchanalai and Sukhothai and are of genuine interest only to the history buff. The **Kamphaeng Phet National Museum** (Wed–Sun 10:00–16:00) offers a good introduction to Thai art from all periods, including the Sukhothai era.

Tak and Mae Sot *

Also on Highway 1, 67km (41 miles) north of Kamphaeng Phet, is Tak, the gateway to the North. The town is situated on the banks of the Ping river, but otherwise has little attraction. Some 80km (50 miles) to the west is **Mae Sot**, on the banks of the Moei river, which forms the border with Burma. Aside from the market, there is little to detain the visitor. The drive from Tak to Mae Sot passes through very attractive hill country.

Central Thailand at a Glance

Kanchanaburi: Buses depart half-hourly 05:00–22:00 from Bangkok's southern bus terminal to Kanchanaburi town. A train departs Bangkok daily at 06:35, arriving Kanchanaburi town at 11:00 and continuing to Nam Tok station.
Ayutthaya: Quickest is by train from Bangkok (90min) – hourly departures.
Lop Buri: Easiest is by train: 3hr from Bangkok; 90min from Ayutthaya.
Sukhothai: Phitsanulok, the easiest access point, is on the Bangkok–Chiang Mai railway line and has daily THAI flights from Bangkok. Sukhothai is included on 'Around Thailand' tours offered by leading Bangkok travel agents.

Kanchanaburi: Bicycles and motorbikes for hire. Most hotels offer sightseeing tours.
Ayutthaya: Locally hired bicycles; *samlor* taxis.
Lop Buri: *Samlors* available, but can be covered on foot.
Sukhothai: Local buses or *songthaews* serve surrounding towns and places of interest. Bicycles can be hired at Sukhothai Historical Park.

Bangkok reservation offices are indicated by BKK Res.
Kanchanaburi
River Kwai, 284/4–6 Saeng Chuto Road, tel 511–184; BKK Res. tel 251–6970
Best in town.

Sam's Place, Song Kwai Road, tel 513–971
Popular medium-priced raft houses.

Ayutthaya
U-Thon Inn, 210 Mu 5, Rotchana Road, tel 242–618. On outskirts of town.
Ayutthaya Guest House, 16/2 Chao Phrom Road, tel 251–468
Popular and cheap.

Lop Buri
Asia Hotel, 1/7–8 Surasak Road, tel 411–892: good location opposite entrance to Narai's palace.

Sukhothai
Northern Palace, 43 Singhawat Road, tel 611–193
Sukhothai's best.
Chinawat Hotel, 1–3 Nikon Kasem Road, tel 611–385
Popular budget choice.

Phitsanulok
Ratchaphruk, 99/9 Phra-Ong-Dum Road, tel 258–788; BKK Res. tel 251–4612
Thep Nakhon, 43/1 Srithamma Traipidok Road, tel 258–507; BKK Res. tel 233–0196

Indra, 103/8 Srithamma

Traipidok Road, tel 259–188

Kamphaeng Phet
Chakangrao, 123/1 Thesa Road, tel 711–315

Tak
Wiang Tak, 25/3 Mahadthai Bamrung Road, tel 511–950; BKK Res. tel 233–2690

Mae Sot
Mae Sot Hills Hotel, 100 Asia Road, tel 532–601
First, 444 Inthakhiri Road, tel 531–233

In **Kanchanaburi** several floating restaurants along the river front. **Isan**, on Saeng Chuto Road, serves good Northeastern food. Around **Sukhothai** food stalls at night markets are good for cheap evening dining. The **Chinawat Hotel** (Sukhothai) restaurant has a good Thai/Western menu. **Phitsanulok** is famous for food stalls selling 'flying vegetables' – stir-fried morning glory which, when cooked, is tossed by the chef to a waiter who catches it (usually) on a plate. Catering to Western tastes in **Mae Sot** is Pim Hut on Tang Kim Chiang Road.

PHITSANULOK	J	F	M	A	M	J	J	A	S	O	N	D
AVERAGE TEMP. °F	77	81	86	88	86	84	84	83	83	83	81	77
AVERAGE TEMP. °C	25	27	30	31	30	29	29	28	28	28	27	25
Hours of Sun Daily	9	9	9	9	8	6	6	5	5	7	8	9
RAINFALL in	1	1	1	2	7	7	8	10	10	6	1	1
RAINFALL mm	6	12	28	51	188	186	195	256	244	157	30	5
Days of Rainfall	1	1	2	3	11	13	14	16	14	10	2	1

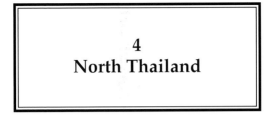

4
North Thailand

Northern Thailand is quite distinct from the Central Plains. Beyond Tak and Sukhothai the lowlands give way to a region of rolling hills and fertile valleys. Teak forests and work elephants are more characteristic than paddy fields and water buffalo. Fruit and vegetables more common to temperate climes are cultivated in addition to rice, while hidden on mountain slopes are opium poppies. Art, architecture and handicrafts are also distinctive, with the unique styles of the North tinged with Burmese influences. The people, too, are different, proud of their separate heritage and distinguished especially by a greater adherence to traditional values and a natural exuberance, readily seen at festivals.

For the traveller the North's attractions are essentially twofold: upland scenery populated by hilltribes, ethnic minorities who more or less maintain traditional lifestyles, and cultural sights attesting to the rich heritage of the former Lanna kingdom.

Hub of the North is **Chiang Mai**, nearly 700km (440 miles) north of Bangkok. This was the ancient Lanna capital, founded in the 13th century, and is today a burgeoning regional centre offering excellent accommodation and other modern facilities amid the well preserved attractions of a historic town. In the far north is **Chiang Rai**, set amid rugged hill country, the famous **Golden Triangle** and the ancient settlement **Chiang Saen** on the banks of the **Mekong river**. To the west is **Mae Hong Son**, an enchanting Shangri-La, and to the east is **Nan**, of great interest though rarely visited.

CLIMATE

The North is subject to the same three-season pattern as Central Thailand, although it is less humid and experiences greater temperature ranges. Night-time temperatures in the hills during the cool season can drop to only a few degrees above freezing. Summer days are hotter than on the Central Plains, while average annual rainfall is about the same, 1300mm (51in).

Opposite: *Cultivated flower fields near Mae Hong Son.*

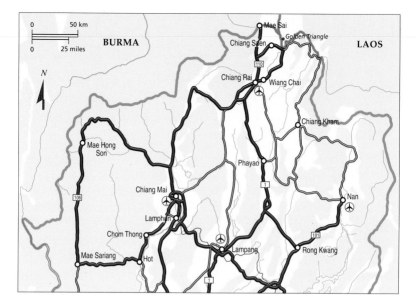

Hilltribes of the North

Not least of the North's attractions are the various hill-tribes who inhabit the jungle-covered mountain slopes. These are people of separate ethnic origin who cling to traditional tribal ways that are fast vanishing.

Opium cultivation in the area sensationally dubbed the 'Golden Triangle' has served to focus popular attention on the hilltribes. However, while some do grow poppies as a cash crop as well as use opium as a traditional cure-all medicine, many others have nothing to do with the drug trade.

An estimated 250,000 to 500,000 tribespeople live in the North, split into seven major groups – Karen, Meo, Akha, Lahu, Lawa, Lisu and Yao. All retain distinct cultures, language and religious beliefs (mostly animistic), though their most obvious distinction is their dress. The women of each tribe – and to a far lesser degree the men – have their own traditional style of colourful, elaborate costume. Handicraft skills, notably in weaving, embroidery and making silver jewellery, are well developed.

DON'T MISS

*** **Chiang Mai**: Ancient temples and 'capital' of the North.
** **Doi Inthanon**: Thailand's highest peak and a national park.
*** **Chiang Rai**: Rugged hill country.
** **Chiang Saen**: Ancient town on banks of Mekong river.
* **Golden Triangle**: Touristy but still worth a visit.
*** **Mae Hong Son**: The quintessential northern experience.
** **Nan**: Off the beaten track.
*** **Northern adventures**: Trekking, mountain biking, river rafting, elephant-back treks.

Being semi-nomadic, the tribespeople are poor and support themselves mostly by slash-and-burn agriculture. Even those who cultivate opium see little of the profits. In an effort to raise living standards and alleviate deep-rooted problems – dire poverty, drugs and environmentally destructive agricultural practices – a number of government and Royal projects have been instigated in recent years. Most are aimed at education and cash-crop substitution programmes, the latter having a notable effect in reducing the extent of opium cultivation.

Above: *Young girls of the Meo hilltribe.*
Below: *Wat Suan Dork, the 'Flower Garden Temple', at Chiang Mai.*

CHIANG MAI

Chiang Mai city is situated mostly on the west bank of the Ping river and lies in a fertile valley ringed by lush green hills. Its layout is dominated by a square moat which encompasses the old city, entered via five now-restored gates: **Chang Puak Gate** in the north; **Ta Pae Gate** in the east; **Chiang Mai Gate** and **Suan Prang Gate**, both in the south; and **Suan Dork Gate** in the west. Today, the city has expanded well beyond the moat and the modern town centre lies to the east between Ta Pae Gate and the river.

Aside from relaxation and shopping for handicrafts, Chiang Mai's main attractions are its temples, which are much older than those in Bangkok and stylistically quite different. Chiang Mai has 36 *wats* standing within the moat and more than 80 throughout the city. For the traveller with limited time, the following are recommended:

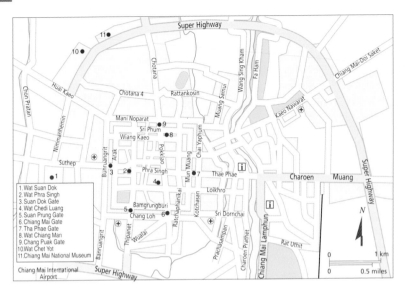

1. Wat Suan Dok
2. Wat Phra Singh
3. Suan Dok Gate
4. Wat Chedi Luang
5. Suan Prung Gate
6. Chiang Mai Gate
7. Tha Phae Gate
8. Wat Chiang Man
9. Chang Puak Gate
10. Wat Chet Yot
11. Chiang Mai National Museum

Street market in the city of Chiang Mai.

Wat Phra Singh ***

On the corner of Singharat and Ratchadamnoen roads, the temple was constructed in 1345 by King Pha Yu, who built the large *chedi* to hold the ashes of his father, King Kam Fu.

Behind the new *viharn* is the *bot* and the famed **Phra Viharn Lai Kam**, one of Chiang Mai's finest northern-style buildings. It enshrines the highly revered image of **Phra Singh Buddha**, sculpted in early Lanna style and originally brought from Chiang Rai. The walls of the *viharn* are decorated with 19th-century mural paintings, the best preserved of their kind in Chiang Mai and fascinating in their details of Northern dress, customs and scenes from daily life a century ago.

Wat Chedi Luang **

On Phra Pokklao Road, Wat Chedi Luang is famous for its massive ruined *chedi*, recently the subject of a controversial restoration project.

The *chedi* was first built in 1401, enlarged to a height of 86m (282ft) by King Tilokaraj in 1454 and then partially destroyed by an earthquake in 1545. Nearby, Chiang Mai's **City Pillar** is housed beneath a gum tree; according to legend, Chiang Mai will prosper only so long as the tree survives.

Wat Chiang Man **

In the northeastern corner of the city on Ratchaphanikai Road, this is probably Chiang Mai's oldest temple. It is reputedly the site of King Mengrai's camp before the city was built.

Most interesting are the temple's several revered Buddha statues, in particular the tiny crystal figure of **Phra Setang Khamani**, reputedly of great antiquity and endowed with rain-making powers, and the stone **Phra Sila**, of Indian origin.

Wat Chet Yot ***

Northwest of the city on the Super Highway, Wat Chet Yot was either built or completely restored by King Tilokaraj in the mid-15th century. It derives its name from the seven (*chet*) spires of its square *chedi*, the unusual design being copied from a temple in Pagan, Burma, itself a copy of the Mahabodhi temple in Bodh Gaya, India. Note the fine stucco celestial figures adorning the sides of the *chedi*. Close to Wat Chet Yot is **Chiang Mai National Museum** (Wed–Sun 09:00–16:00), which presents an interesting if uninspired collection of Lanna exhibits.

Wat Suan Dork and Wat Umong **

Wat Suan Dork, the 'Flower Garden Temple' off Suthep Road a short distance west of Suan Dork Gate, is a historically important temple with a huge bell-shaped *chedi*, but it is architecturally unattractive.

A more evocative temple in the same area is Wat Umong, one of Chiang Mai's oldest temple monasteries, with underground cells for meditation. Much of the original building is in ruins, although a visit is worthwhile for the tranquil forest-like setting (access is tricky, via a winding lane off Suthep Road).

DOI INTHANON NATIONAL PARK

Some 80km (50 miles) south-west of Chiang Mai is Thailand's highest peak at 2565m (8415ft). The area is designated as a national park and offers a readily accessible slice of typical northern countryside, complete with hilltribe villages. In the vicinity are three picturesque water-falls – Mae Klang, Vachiratarn and Mae Ya – which are popular picnic areas. The nearest main town to Doi Inthanon is Chom Thong, where **Wat Phra That Si Chom Thong** is one of the finest Buddhist monu-ments outside Chiang Mai.

Excursions from Chiang Mai
Doi Suthep ***

The most popular short excursion from Chiang Mai is to this imposing mountain some 15km (10 miles) west of town and famous for **Wat Phrathat**, perched close to the summit. The temple (reached either by a flight of 290 steps or by funicular) comprises an imposing gilded *chedi*, originally erected in the late 14th century, two sanctuaries and cloisters dating from the 16th century (since restored on several occasions). Lavish and ornate decoration is matched by magnificent panoramic views of the surrounding countryside.

The site of Wat Phrathat, according to legend, was chosen in the late 14th century when King Ku Na was seeking a repository for some holy relics. These were placed in a howdah on the back of an elephant which was then set free to wander at will. The animal proceed-ed to climb Doi Suthep and near the top it stopped, trumpeted and turned round three times before kneel-ing, indicating that this was the chosen spot.

The road continues beyond the foot of Doi Suthep and after 4km (2¹/₂ miles) reaches **Phuping Palace**, the Royal Family's northern residence whose gardens are open to the public Fri–Sun 08:00–16:00. A further 3km (2 miles) from the palace is **Doi Pui**, an authentic but unfor-tunately commercialized Hmong hilltribe village.

Lamphun **

One of the most pleasant excursions and a rewarding trip for history enthusiasts is to Lamphun, 26km (16 miles) south of Chiang Mai. Part of the road is lined with huge trees which give an idea of how densely forested the area once was. Lamphun is the site of **Haripunchai**, the capital of a Mon kingdom founded in AD660 and defeated by King Mengrai in the late 13th century. The small modern town is unremarkable except for **Wat Phra That Haripunchai**, superb in architectural beauty and historical interest. The temple was originally built in 1044, although the various buildings in the large com-pound, dominated by a 50m (164ft) *chedi*, are of varying

THA THON AND KOK RIVER

The tiny settlement of Tha Thon, located 175km (110 miles) north of Chiang Mai on the Kok river close to the Burmese border, is the hop-ping-off point for the river trip to Chiang Rai. This splen-did journey can be made either by longtail boat (daily departures at 12:30) in 4–5hr, or by raft in 3 days (2 nights). Wild scenery and hill-tribe villages make for an unforgettable journey. Tha Thon is 5hr by bus from Chiang Mai and has some surprisingly good accommo-dation.

dates. Near the temple is the small but well planned **National Museum** (Wed–Sun 09:00–12:00, 13:00–16:00).

On the west side of town is **Wat Ku Kut** (also known as **Wat Chama Devi**), an important temple for its two ancient *chedis*, dating probably from the early 13th century and regarded as the only surviving examples of Dvaravati architecture. The taller of the two, **Suwan Chang Kot**, is in the form of a stepped pyramid 21m (69ft) high and 15.4m (51ft) wide, while the smaller **Ratana Chedi** is 11.5m (38ft) high and octagonal in shape.

LAMPANG

Despite its status as a moderately large provincial centre and transport hub, Lampang, 100km (62 miles) southeast of Chiang Mai, preserves traces of its past, although the town is not as old-world as its famous horse-drawn carriages might suggest. None the less, a trip is recommended if time permits. On the northern edge of town, on the right bank of the Wang river, **Wat Phra Kaeo Don Tao** is a fine temple complex displaying both Thai and Burmese architectural styles. According to legend, the **Emerald Buddha** was enshrined here for 32 years in the mid-15th century. Among other city temples are **Wat Pha Fang**, with a tall *chedi* unusually surrounded by seven small chapels, and **Wat Sri Chum**, a good example of Burmese-style religious architecture. The most magnificent temple in the area, however, is **Wat Phra That Lampang Luang**, dating back to AD496 but completely rebuilt in the 18th century. Located off Highway 1 some 15km (10 miles) south of Lampang, it is

The temple compound at Wat Phra That Haripunchai, Lamphun, includes a school for Buddhist monks.

difficult to reach by public transport, but the effort is more than worth it as this walled temple is one of the finest and best-preserved examples of Lanna style.

An excursion to Lampang can also include a visit to the **Young Elephant Training Centre**, 25km (15 miles) west of town on Highway 11. This is the most authentic of several elephant camps giving shows of how young elephants are trained for work in the teak forests.

CHIANG RAI

King Mengrai founded Chiang Rai in 1262. Some 35 years later he moved 182km (113 miles) south to bigger and better things at Chiang Mai. That, briefly, sums up the history of the capital of Thailand's northernmost province. Overshadowed by Chiang Mai, it has forever been a backwater, sprawling lazily on the right bank of the Kok river. Things are set to change, however, as Chiang Rai becomes recognized as an excellent base for exploring the Far North, while the surrounding countryside holds some of its most spectacular attractions, all of which can be reached in easy day trips from the city.

Wat Phra Kaeo, on Trairat Road, has a late Lanna-period chapel and a few fine bronze images, though it is mostly famous for its restored *chedi* which, according to legend, was where Bangkok's famous statue of the **Emerald Buddha** was discovered in 1436.

Young elephants receiving a bath after giving a demonstration at their training camp.

Wat Phra Singh, on nearby Singhakai Road, used to enshrine the important image of **Phra Buddha Si Hing**; the original has now been moved to Chiang Mai and a copy sits in its place.

Wat Ngam Muang, sited on a small hill west of Wat Phra Kaeo and reached by a short flight of *naga*-flanked steps, has an ancient brick *chedi* which is the reliquary for the remains of King Mengrai. It was first erected in 1318, though the structure seen today is of later construction.

Wat Doi Tung, on a hill north of Wat Ngam Muang, comprises a *viharn* and a Burmese-style *chedi*. The location commands views of the Kok river and tradition has it that King Mengrai first surveyed the site of the city here.

For a glimpse of Chiang Rai's traditional character, the morning market near **Wat Mung Muang** should not be missed; catch it at its liveliest before 07:00.

Excursions from Chiang Rai

• **Doi Mae Salong and Doi Tung**: Two high forested peaks of great natural beauty, located 30km (20 miles) and 40km (25 miles) north of Chiang Rai, respectively. Roads wind upwards through the corrugated slopes dotted with hilltribe villages to the summits of both mountains, affording breathtaking views east to the Mekong and Laos, and west to the hills of Burma. Topping Doi Mae Salong, the wilder of the two peaks, is a village inhabited by former members of the Kuomintang army and their descendants. Doi Tung is by contrast tamer and has been extensively developed. At the summit, however, is the lovely little temple of **Wat Phra Thai Doi Tung**, with twin *chedis* erected to enshrine relics of the Buddha in 911. It is an especially sacred spot not only for Thais but also for Laotians and Shans from Burma.

• **Chiang Saen**: A charming little market town on the banks of the Mekong northeast of Chiang Rai, Chiang Saen is the site of an ancient and once powerful settlement, as witnessed by a number of historic monuments, most notably the splendid *chedi* of **Wat Pa Sak**, built in 1295, and the ruins of **Wat Phra That Chom Kitti**. Together with a handful of other ruins, these afford ample sightseeing possibilities. Nor should the small but worthwhile museum be overlooked (Wed–Sun 09:00–16:00).

• **Golden Triangle**: A few kilometres upstream from

HILL TREKKING

As the more traditional villages are far from towns, trekking is the best way of visiting the hilltribes, although mountain biking is becoming an increasingly popular option. The most rewarding trekking areas are around Chiang Rai and Mae Hong Son, and 3- or 4-day trips organized by reliable travel agents are recommended. Choose your tour carefully: irresponsible trekking companies both prostitute hilltribe culture and offer little security for the trekker. You can obtain a list of reputable agencies from the Tourism Authority of Thailand in Chiang Mai.

Chiang Saen is the confluence of the Mekong and Ruak rivers, forming the border between Thailand, Burma and Laos, the spot known as the 'Golden Triangle'. This famous juncture is best viewed by climbing up the small hill to **Wat Phra That Phu Khao**. Unfortunately, the area is cluttered with hotels, guesthouses and downmarket souvenir stalls, effectively destroying any intriguing atmosphere.

The name 'Golden Triangle' also refers to a vastly greater area of these three countries which produces two-thirds of the world's opium output – around 2400 tonnes annually. Although the signposted 'Golden Triangle' near Chiang Saen on the banks of the Mekong lies in the heart of opium country, it suffers gross tourism development – here, instead of mule trains and drug traffickers, are tour buses and souvenir touts.

MAE HONG SON

Spectacularly cradled amid mist-shrouded forested mountains, Mae Hong Son is arguably the North's most enchanting excursion option. Lying up against the Burmese border northwest of Chiang Mai, this sleepy little town combines surprisingly well developed tourism facilities with a pleasing sense of isolation.

The town can easily be reached by THAI's daily direct flight from Bangkok, or in a short hop from Chiang Mai. By road Mae Hong Son is 370km (230 miles) from Chiang Mai and the drive (about 8–9hr) is a thrilling rollercoaster ride as the road winds its way up, down and around the mountains. The small town of Mae Sariang serves as halfway halt.

On arrival, the immediate attraction of Mae Hong Son is a feeling of tranquillity. A distinct character is preserved not only by old wooden houses and ageing Burmese-style temples, but also by the people, mainly Shans and a scattering of Karen, Meo, Lisu and Lahu tribespeople. To see the town at its liveliest, a visit to the morning market is a must. Here, between 06:00 and 08:00, hilltribe people mix with townsfolk and there is an untypical buzz of activity around colourful stalls loaded with fruit, vegetables, spices, meats, clothes and household goods.

Dominating the western edge of town is **Doi Kong Mu**, a 424m (1391ft) peak topped by **Wat Phrathat Doi Kong Mu**. The two *chedis*, erected in 1860 and 1874 respectively, and the several surrounding images are fascinating, but the real reward is the magnificent bird's eye view of the narrow fertile valley and encircling mountains. At the foot of Doi Kong Mu, **Wat Phra Non** houses a 12m (39ft) long Burmese-style reclining Buddha image.

Bordering the town's small but extremely picturesque lake are **Wat Chong Kam** and **Wat Chong Klang**. Both temples display typical Burmese-style architecture, and Wat Chong Klang is notable for its collection of Burmese wooden dolls, the tallest about 1m (3ft) high, representing figures from one of the traditional stories about the Buddha's previous lives.

Wat Hua Wieng, near the market, looks even more dilapidated than usual for the typically tottering wood-and-corrugated-iron architecture of Mae Hong Son's Burmese-style temples, but it does enshrine a fine brass seated Buddha, a copy of a statue in Mandalay.

Attractions beyond Mae Hong Son are numerous. Besides the overall spectacular mountain scenery, natural sights within easy distance of town include **Tham Pla** (Fish Cave), **Pha Sua waterfall** and **Tham Lod cave**, a splendid cavern with a stream running through it. There are also numerous hill-tribe villages. Trekking and excursions by jeep, elephant and river transport are organized by tour agents (concentrated on Khunlum Praphat Road) and resort hotels.

Intensive farming in a fertile valley near Mae Hong Son.

Sinuous stone nagas *flanking a stairway at Wat Pumin.*

NAN

Lying 745km (463 miles) north of Bangkok, on the eastern edge of the northern region, Nan is largely off the tourist map. As well as some interesting temples, it benefits from a pleasant location amid some splendid surrounding scenery.

Founded as an independent state in the 13th century, Nan became part of the Lanna kingdom in 1450. From 1558 it was under Burmese sovereignty and, after the foreign occupiers were finally expelled in 1786, it pledged allegiance to the nation's new capital, Bangkok, although its own ruling dynasty was allowed to persist with certain privileges of autonomy until 1931.

The best starting point is the **National Museum** (Wed–Sun 09:00–16:00), centrally located in a former palace. Its prize possession is a black elephant tusk, reputedly brought to Nan some 300 years ago.

Wat Chang Kham Vora Viharn, located directly opposite the museum, derives its name from its *chedi*, originally built in 1406, which has a base adorned with seven elephant (*chang*) buttresses on each side. The main attraction, though, is a superb 145cm (57in) gold statue of the walking Buddha housed in the monks' residence.

Wat Pumin, just beyond Wat Chang Kham Vora Viharn on the opposite side of the road, is Nan's most famous temple. The main preaching hall dates from the late 16th century and follows an untypical cruciform pattern, with steps leading up to exquisitely carved entrance doors on each of the four sides. Two of the stairways are flanked by balustrades in the form of *nagas*. The interior is dominated by a centrepiece of four Buddha statues facing the four cardinal points, while the walls are covered with fine mural paintings.

Wat Phra That Chae Haeng is an ancient walled temple located east of the river 2km (1½ miles) from town and occupying an elevated site reached by a *naga*-flanked approach. It is a most imposing monument dominated by a 55m (180ft) *chedi* covered with gilded copper plaques, while the preaching hall has an impressive three-tiered, five-level tiled roof.

North Thailand at a Glance

GETTING THERE

Chiang Mai: Several daily planes (1hr), trains (13hr) and buses (14hr) from Bangkok.
Chiang Rai: Daily direct THAI flight from Bangkok (80min). Daily and overnight air-conditioned buses from Bangkok (10hr). Daily flights (50min) and buses (4hr) from Chiang Mai.
Mae Hong Son: Daily THAI flight from Bangkok via Chiang Mai (2hr 10min) and twice-daily flights from Chiang Mai (30min). Air-conditioned buses from Chiang Mai (8–9hr).
Nan: Bus or plane from Chiang Mai or Bangkok.

GETTING AROUND

Chiang Mai: Easiest around town is *tuk tuk* or *songthaew*.
Chiang Rai: Bicycle *samlors* or *songthaews*. Hire cars, jeeps, motorbikes available.
Mae Hong Son: Some *samlors*; also motorbike taxis and *songthaews*. Jeep/motorbike hire.

WHERE TO STAY

Chiang Mai
Chiang Mai Orchid, 100–102 Huai Kaeo Road, tel 222–099, BKK Res. tel 245–3973, fax 246–2136; top-class/outskirts.
Royal Princess, 112 Chang Klang Road, tel 281–033, BKK Res. tel 236–0450, fax 236–6400 High standards; central location.
Thai Charoen, 164–6 Thapae Road, tel 236–640 Central, cheap but noisy .
Top North Guesthouse, 15 Soi 2, Moon Muang Road, tel 213–900 Typical Chiang Mai guesthouse.

Chiang Rai
Dusit Island, 1129 Kraisorasit Road, tel 715–777, fax 715–801, BKK Res. tel 236–0450, fax 236–6400 Lovely river island location.
Rimkok Resort, 6 Moo 4, Chiang Rai–Tathorn Road, Rimkok District, tel 715–858, fax 715–859, BKK Res. tel 279–0102, fax 278–4878 Riverside setting.
Wangcome Hotel, 869/90 Pemavipat Road, tel 711–800, fax 712–973, BKK Res. tel 252–7760, fax 254–4255
Wiang Inn Hotel, 893 Phaholyothin, tel 711–543, fax 711–877, BKK Res. tel 235–4030 ext 241 Both typical provincial first-class properties in town centre.
Golden Triangle Inn, 590 Phaholyothin Road, tel 711–339 Inexpensive; very comfortable; fine restaurant; friendly staff.
Mae Hong Son
Tara Mae Hong Sorn, 149 Moo 8, Tambon Pang Moo, tel 611–473, fax 611–252, BKK Res. tel 254–0023
Holiday Inn, 114/5–7 Khunlum Praphat Road, tel 611–108, fax 611–231, BKK Res. tel 254–2614 Both excellent; town outskirts.
Mae Hong Son Resort, 24 Ban Huey Daer, tel/fax 611–504 Rustic, with riverside setting.

Rim Nam Klang Doi Resort, 108 T. Pabong Muang, tel 612–142, fax 612–086 Riverside resort with excellent restaurant.
Baiyoke Chalet Hotel, 90 Khunlum Praphat Road, tel 611–486, BKK Res. tel 251–1847 Best in town centre; cheap.
Nan
Thewarat (Dhevaraj), 466 Sumon Thewarat Road, tel 710–094 Provincial first class.
Suk Kasem, 29–31 Ananworaritdet Road, tel 710–141 Cheap, shabby but acceptable.

WHERE TO EAT

Chiang Mai: Wide choice. Good Thai food at the open-air **Aroon Rai. The Pub** is a pub-cum-restaurant with Continental cuisine.
Chiang Rai: Thai food at the **Chiang Rai Island Restaurant. The Hawnariga** is an inexpensive open-front Thai restaurant.
Mae Hong Son: On Khunlum Praphat Road, good Thai food at **Fern** (no. 87) and extensive Chinese/Thai/Western menu at **Khai Muk** (no. 71).
Nan: Swiss-run **Tiptop** (Mahawong Road) serves Italian, Swiss, Thai dishes.

CHIANG MAI	J	F	M	A	M	J	J	A	S	O	N	D
AVERAGE TEMP. °F	69	73	78	84	83	81	80	80	80	78	75	70
AVERAGE TEMP. °C	21	23	26	29	28	27	27	27	27	26	23	21
Hours of Sun Daily	8	8	8	8	8	8	8	5	5	7	8	8
RAINFALL in	1	1	1	2	6	5	6	10	9	5	2	1
RAINFALL mm	6	5	13	30	158	131	160	236	227	122	52	19
Days of Rainfall	1	1	2	6	15	17	19	21	17	11	6	2

5
Northeast Thailand

The Northeast has been largely untouched by the tourism boom. Here it is possible to escape the common run and glimpse a traditional Thailand that is fast vanishing.

I-san, as the region is known in Thai, is the least changed part of the country – it is also the poorest, with an agriculture-based economy blighted by low-yield soil and unpredictable rains. Yet in spite of a relatively low standard of living – or perhaps because of it – cultural traditions are here better preserved than elsewhere. This, together with pronounced Lao and Khmer influences, reinforces distinct regional characteristics – dialect, customs, food, festivals, folk dances and music in particular. Comprising a vast, semi-arid plateau, the Northeast is bordered in the north and east by the **Mekong river**, marking the boundary with Laos, and in the south by the **Dongrak mountains** which divide Thailand from Cambodia. The area covers roughly one-third of Thailand's land mass and contains about one-third of the population. Although village life is characteristic, main towns such as **Khorat**, **Khon Kaen** and **Ubon Ratchathani** are among the most populous in Thailand.

Aside from its welcome breath of fresh air – literal as well as figurative – the Northeast is most remarkable for its Khmer temple ruins. Otherwise it is an area of cumulative interest, of slight but intriguing historical, cultural and scenic sights ideally combined in a leisurely tour by car or motorbike (most conveniently hired in Bangkok or the I-san gateway town of Khorat).

CLIMATE

The hot season in the Northeast is extremely uncomfortable – the mercury pushes 40˚C (104˚F) and above, while the sight of a parched landscape makes it seem even hotter. During the Nov-Feb cool season it is greener and there is more water in the Mekong. On the other hand, I-san's most thrilling festival, the Rocket Festival at Yasothon, is held in May.

Opposite: *Meeting of two rivers, the Mekong (left) and the Mun (right).*

DON'T MISS

**Khao Yai: Thailand's first and most popular national park.
***Phimai: Extensive Khmer temple complex.
***Phanom Rung: Khmer temple in spectacular hilltop location.
***Mekong: World's 12th longest river.
**Nong Khai: Charming Mekong town and gateway to Laos.
**Ban Chiang: Prehistoric archaeological site.
**Khon Kaen: Silk-weaving centre.

Numerous colourful and exuberant annual festivals traditional to I-san are additional attractions, and you can consider yourself fortunate if a major event coincides with your visit.

We describe below a three-day tour of four unmissable Khmer temples, and a circular route for travellers who prefer a more comprehensive view of the region.

KHAO YAI, KHORAT AND KHMER TEMPLES

A comfortable three-day trip from Bangkok permits sightseeing at four of I-san's best Khmer ruins, plus a side-trip to Khao Yai National Park. The base is Khorat, 260km (160 miles) northeast of Bangkok. The itinerary is: day 1: Bangkok/Khao Yai–Khorat; day 2: Khorat/Phanom Rung and Muang Tam temples/Khorat; day 3: Khorat/Phanom Wan and Phimai temples/Bangkok.

Khao Yai National Park **

Located roughly midway between Bangkok and Khorat, Khao Yai is one of Thailand's finest national parks, possessing great natural beauty, comparatively plentiful

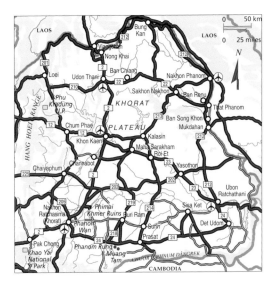

wildlife and large tracts of seasonal tropical forest. Access is via a turning off Highway 2 near the small town of **Pak Chong**, 58km (36 miles) northwest of Saraburi. The park covers 2172 sq km (840 sq miles) of protected forest, jungle and grassland spread over rolling hills and mountains (the highest, **Khao Laem**, is 1328m/4357ft).

Haew Suwat, one of several lovely waterfalls in Khao Yai National Park.

The area is traversed by paved roads, and there are also a dozen marked walking trails. Vantage points afford spectacular panoramic views, while waterfalls add to the considerable scenic attraction. A wildlife population of at least 25 of the larger mammals includes elephants, tigers, leopards, Asiatic black bears, Malayan sun bears, barking deer and sambar deer. Easier to spot are Khao Yai's over 300 species of birds and numerous butterflies.

Khorat

As a burgeoning commercial centre, Khorat (more correctly called Nakhon Ratchasima) is not typical of I-san as a whole. Sightseeing options amount to nothing more remarkable than the **Thao Suranari Monument**, which honours the wife of a Khorat deputy governor who saved the city from a Lao attack in 1826, and **Wat Sala Loi** ('Temple of the Floating Pavilion'), where the chapel is in the shape of a Chinese junk. The city does, however, offer a reasonably acceptable standard of accommodation.

Richly carved stonework at the ancient Khmer temple of Prasat Muang Tam.

Phanom Rung and Prasat Muang Tam ★★★

Open daily 08:00–17:00. Both ancient Khmer temples lie about 120km (75 miles) east of Khorat. Dating mostly from the 12th century, Phanom Rung is a comparatively well preserved, though restored, temple complex which is all the more impressive for its splendid hilltop location. The sanctuary is approached via an imposing paved avenue and a grand stone stairway, while the principal buildings within the walled compound comprise a chambered gateway, and a square-based sanctuary tower with entrances and antechambers at the four cardinal points. Also noteworthy are the pediments and carved lintels of interior and exterior doorways, and the decorative friezes on walls and pillars.

Prasat Muang Tam, with 10th-century foundations, thus predating Phanom Rung, lies at the foot of the hill. Badly ruined and given a melting Daliesque appearance through land subsidence, it is none the less complete in its architectural symbolism. At the centre of the walled compound is a now collapsed central *prang*, surrounded by four smaller towers, and in the four corners are L-shaped ponds. The site is rich in carved stonework, though its immediate attraction springs from its romantic air.

The foundations of Prasat Muang Tam date from the 10th century.

Prasat Phanom Wan and Phimai ★★★

Open daily 08:30–16:00. Situated 15km (9 miles) north of Khorat along Highway 2 and a further 5km (3 miles) down a signposted turn-off to the right, Prasat Phanom Wan is one of the smallest and least visited of I-san's main temples. The attractive 1000-year-old sanctuary faces a modern monastic building and otherwise stands in an isolated walled compound. The main building is in

Phanom Rung owes its well preserved air to recent restoration work.

fairly good condition and comprises a vaulted chamber leading to a rectangular-based tower. Untypically, the temple is still in use and enshrines several Buddha images, the sight of which adds a sense of religious awe to the ruins.

Phimai, largest of the four temple complexes, lies beyond Phanom Wan, about 30km (18 miles) further along Highway 2 and 12km (7¹/₂ miles) off to the right. Dating from the end of the 11th century, the original settlement at Phimai occupied an artificial island on the Mun river and a number of remains are scattered about the present town. The principal sanctuary tower, however, stands in its own extensive walled compound. Finely proportioned and with adjoining antechamber and porticos on three sides, it is a splendid monument in spite of having been restored with dubious accuracy.

Other impressive remains are the *prangs* of flanking sanctuaries in the inner courtyard by the southern gateway, and four corner ceremonial ponds in the outer courtyard. On the left as you cross the Mun river to enter the town is an open-air museum (Wed–Sun 08:30–16:30) with a fine collection of carved lintels from Phimai and other Khmer sites in the Northeast.

FESTIVALS

The local culture of the Northeast is vividly witnessed in many traditional festivals that punctuate the unchanging seasonal cycle of ploughing, planting and reaping. Among the most spectacular events are:

Yasothon Rocket Festival: Held in May with homemade rockets fired to assure the arrival of the annual rains.

Candle Festival: Held at Ubon Ratchathani to celebrate the beginning of the Buddhist Rains Retreat in July. Colourful floats process around town bearing huge and elaborately styled wax candles.

Elephant Round-Up: Elephant extravaganza at Surin in Nov in which elephants demonstrate their work skills. The culmination of the event is an exciting mock battle with elephants decked in old-fashioned war regalia.

NORTHEAST CIRCULAR TOUR

The following route heads north from Khorat and then swings east and south, paralleling the Mekong, before turning west to Ubon Ratchathani and back through Surin to Khorat. Allow a minimum of 4–5 days.

Khon Kaen **

This modern university town 190km (120 miles) north of Khorat is a regional centre with good accommodation, although the only sight really worth seeking out is the excellent museum (Wed–Sun 09:00–12:00, 13:00–16:00). In December Khon Kaen is the venue for the annual Silk Fair. Silk-weaving is a renowned I-san handicraft and the whole process from silkworm to loom can be seen at the village of **Chonnabot**, about 50km (30 miles) south of Khon Kaen.

Ban Chiang **

About 50km (30 miles) along Highway 22 east of **Udon Thani**, a large commercial hub some 120km (75 miles) north of Khon Kaen, is the village of Ban Chiang, set amid typical I-san rural scenery. The area became famous in the early 1970s when prehistoric finds yielded evidence of early human habitation which set archaeologists rethinking the pattern of civilization. The finds, including skeletons, tools and distinctively decorated pottery, have been dated as over 5000 years old. This predates sites in China and Mesopotamia as the earliest known evidence of an agrarian, bronze-making civilization. Excavation work at Ban Chiang has long been completed, but in the compound of **Wat Poh Si Nai**, on the far side of the village, two pits have been left open to display archaeological finds *in situ*. Ban Chiang also has a small but informative museum (Wed–Sun 09:00–12:00, 13:00–16:00).

Loei *

The provincial capital of Loei, 145km (90 miles) west of Udon Thani, is unexceptional, although the province itself has some wonderfully scenic countryside. Notable among several preserved sites are: **Phu Kradung National Park**, a tabletop plateau at an average elevation of 1300m (4265ft) with temperate-clime flora, some 80km (50 miles) south of Loei town; and **Phu Luang Wildlife Sanctuary**, also a high plateau, about 50km (30 miles) south of town, with comparatively abundant wildlife, including elephant and deer.

Nong Khai **

On the banks of the Mekong 56km (35 miles) north of Udon, Nong Khai is a small but lively border town of considerable charm. It is the hopping-off point for entry into Laos via the Thai–Lao Friendship Bridge, the first span across the Mekong outside China. Nothing is more pleasant than simply watching the river flow by, although **Wat Pho Chai**, on Prajak Road, has a curious attraction. The temple's presiding Buddha image, so legend has it, was shipwrecked in the Mekong during a storm but miraculously the 1.5m (5ft) gold statue floated ashore. Wat Khaek has an extensive garden of weird concrete statuary blending themes from Buddhist and Hindu mythology. Further afield, 22km (13 miles) southwest of Nong Khai, **Wat Phra That Bang Phuan** is a venerable and highly revered temple in a tranquil rural setting.

Nakhon Phanom

From Nong Khai, the Mekong and the Thai border which it marks run east and then south. The first town of note is Nakhon Phanom, 242km (150 miles) from Nong Khai. Its greatest attraction is stunning views across the Mekong to the mountains of Laos.

That Phanom **

This tiny settlement 54km (34 miles) south of Nakhon Phanom is the site of **Wat That Phanom**, the northeast's most sacred Buddhist shrine, as illustrated by the huge attendance at the temple's annual fair (late Jan/early Feb). Wat That Phanom is dominated by a 57m (187ft) Lao-style spire, known as a *that*, which collapsed in 1975 after four days of monsoon rains. According to local leg-

> ### *MUTMEE SILK*
>
> Unique to the Northeast, *mutmee* silk is generally accepted as Thailand's best – and most expensive – fabric. Hand-woven from filaments of uniform size and texture, it is distinguished by its thread, which is tie-dyed in several colours, and its traditional intricate patterns.

Bizarre statuary in the extraordinary religious 'theme park' of Wat Khaek near Nong Khai.

Stilt dwellings on the Mun river at Ubon Ratchathani.

end, it was believed that if the spire should fall, so too would Laos. A few months after the disaster Laos was taken over by the communist Pathet Lao. The spire was subsequently rebuilt by the Thai Fine Arts Department.

Mukdahan

Located 53km (33 miles) south of That Phanom, Mukdahan is the last main Thai town on the Mekong. Its principal interest is its setting, although near the village of **Ban Song Khon**, 25km (15 miles) north, is the memorial site of the only Thais to be beatified. Seven Catholics shot here in December 1940, accused of aiding the French during a border conflict, were proclaimed 'Blessed Martyrs' in a 1989 papal decree.

Ubon Ratchathani

Below Mukdahan the main highway leaves the Mekong and heads 160km (100 miles) southwest to Ubon Ratchathani, a major provincial centre located on the banks of the Mun river, a Mekong tributary. **Wat Thung Si Muang** boasts a fine wooden library raised on stilts over a pond, and a small *bot* with some charming mural paintings. **Wat Phra That Nong Bua**, on the outskirts of town, is notable for its impressive modern *stupa* modelled on that of the Mahabodhi temple at Bodh Gaya, India, and decorated with scenes from the *Jataka* tales.

An excursion east from Ubon leads 100km (65 miles) to Khong Chiam and the confluence of the Mun and Mekong rivers, an attractive spot known locally as **'Two-Colour River'** because of the contrast between the brown Mekong and the relatively clear water of the Mun. Nearby is **Pha Taem**, a sheer cliff with prehistoric rock paintings dated to between 1000 and 3000 years. The crude sketches showing elephants and fish, as well as hand prints, are evocative rather than impressive.

From Ubon it is 310km (195 miles) west back to Khorat. Among several Khmer temple ruins along the Thai–Cambodian border is **Khao Phra Viharn**. This spectacular hilltop monument belongs to Cambodia but is accessible from the Thai side of the border.

ELEPHANT HUNTERS

The village of **Ta Klang**, some 50km (31 miles) north of Surin town, is a settlement of Suay people, a tribal minority once famed for uncanny skill in hunting and training elephants. Today, the number of mahouts and elephants have both declined drastically, but some of the skill of the Suay can be seen at the **Elephant Round-Up**, an annual pageant held at Surin in Nov.

Northeast Thailand at a Glance

GETTING THERE

THAI run daily flights from Bangkok to Khorat, Khon Kaen, Udon Thani and Ubon Ratchathani. Bangkok Airways flies from Bangkok to Loei. (Most flights about 1hr.) Rail links from Bangkok via Khorat (4hr): southern route to Ubon Ratchathani (10+hr) and northern route to Nong Khai (11hr). Long-distance buses from Bangkok to all major towns.

GETTING AROUND

Local bus services are comprehensive, but best is to hire a car or motorbike.

WHERE TO STAY

Khorat
Royal Princess, 1137 Suranarai Road, tel 256–629, fax 256–601, BKK Res. tel 236–0450, fax 238–4797 International standard.
Chomsurang Hotel, 2701/2 Mahatthai Road, tel 257–088. Traditional favourite.
Sripattana Hotel, 3551/5, Suranaree Road, tel 242–944 Good; medium-priced.
Siri Hotel, 688–690 Pho–Klang Road, tel 242–831 Good location; inexpensive.
Khon Kaen
Kosa Hotel, 250–52 Si Chan Road, tel 225–014, fax 225–013 Good provincial first-class.
Roma Hotel, 48/6–50/2 Klang Muang Road, tel 236–276 Best of several modestly priced hotels along this road.

Udon Thani
Charoen Hotel, 549 Phosri Road, tel 221–331 Good provincial first-class.
Queen Hotel, 6–8 Udon–Dusadi Road, tel 221–451 Popular budget hotel.
Nong Khai
Nong Khai Grand Thani, 589 Mu 5, Nong Khai–Phon Phisai Road, tel 420–033, fax 412–026, BKK Res. tel 236–0450, fax 238–4797 Best in town.
Phanthawi, 1241 Hai Soke Road, tel 411–568 Medium-priced.
Sukhaphen, 1103–5 Banthoeng Chit Road, tel 411–894 Old renovated wooden Chinese hotel; inexpensive.
Nakhon Phanom
Nakhon Phanom Hotel, 403 Aphiban Bancha Road, tel 511–455 Comfortable; friendly.
River Inn, 137 Sunthan Wichit Road, tel 511–305 Mediocre, but superb river views; good restaurant.
Surin
Phetkasem, 104 Chitbamrung Road, tel 511–274 Best in town; medium-priced.
Ubon Ratchathani
Patumrat Hotel, 173 Chayangkun Road, tel 241–501

Typical provincial first-class.
Tokyo Hotel, 178 Upparat Road, tel 241–739 Popular; inexpensive.

WHERE TO EAT

Safe bets are night-market foodstalls and other restaurants that seem popular with the locals. Try:
Khorat: **VFW (Veterans of Foreign Wars) Restaurant** (nest to Siri Hotel) is a funky place for steaks, hamburgers, pizzas, etc.
Udon Thani: Some restaurants at top end of Prajak Road serve good local food.
Nong Khai: **New Panya Pochana**, popular riverside restaurant near the ferry pier.
Dukada Bakery (Meechai Road) serves Western breakfasts plus pastries and Thai foods.
Nakhon Phanom: **Pla Beuk Thong** (Phochana Road), riverside restaurant.
Mukdahan: **Phai Rim Khong** (Samlarn Chai Khong Road) offers good Thai food by riverside. **Suwa Blend** for coffeeshop-style Thai and Western food.
Ubon Ratchathani: **Khun Piak** (just out of town on road to Yasothon) is a pleasant sala-style I-san place.

KHORAT	J	F	M	A	M	J	J	A	S	O	N	D
AVERAGE TEMP. °F	76	80	84	86	86	84	84	82	82	80	77	74
AVERAGE TEMP. °C	24	27	29	30	30	29	29	28	28	27	25	23
Hours of Sun Daily	9	8	9	9	7	6	6	5	5	6	7	8
RAINFALL in	1	1	2	3	6	4	5	5	10	6	1	1
RAINFALL mm	5	23	42	66	149	107	123	131	244	153	30	3
Days of Rainfall	1	2	3	6	12	9	11	11	15	9	3	1

6
The East Coast

Thailand's East Coast, an angled corner reaching some 500km (310 miles) from the mouth of the Chao Phraya river around to the Cambodian border, offers a wealth of attractions ranging from the ridiculous to the sublime. On the one hand is **Pattaya**, formerly the Kingdom's premier beach resort but now a victim of developers' greed; on the other hand are the tranquil tropical islands of the **Ko Chang archipelago**, as yet unspoilt. In between are pleasant, unexceptional spots for a quiet time by the sea, while inland are pretty views of green hills and fruit orchards. None of the beaches is as good as those in the South, but they do have the advantage of being within a 2–3hr drive from Bangkok along a modern highway.

Pattaya is now more of a fun city than a true beach resort. Increasingly it is becoming a service station for the ambitious Eastern Seaboard economic development programme, which so far has spawned industrial estates and port facilities at **Laem Chabang** and **Map Ta Phut**. Herein lies the future, but Pattaya can still be recommended as a resort quite unlike any other.

BANGKOK TO BANG SAEN

The **Bangna–Trat Highway** offers fast but characterless road access to the East Coast; the old **Sukhumvit Highway** provides an alternative route which, if not picturesque, does display vestiges of local colour.

Bangkok's heavy traffic is left behind once beyond **Samut Prakan**, and a *klong* runs down the left-hand side

CLIMATE

The East Coast has the same hottest, coolest and wettest months as Bangkok, but, as with other coastal areas, the temperatures tend to be more uniform year round. Parts of the region, notably Ko Samet, Ko Chang and Cambodia border areas, are in the **malarial zone** and, while prophylactics are mostly ineffective, use of insect repellent and mosquito nets is advisable.

Opposite: *The wide blue sweep of Pattaya Bay speckled with small pleasure boats.*

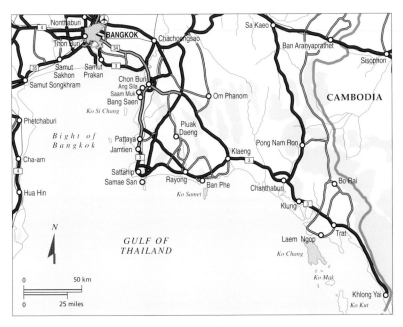

of the road. Small, old-style houses on stilts with 'butter-fly' fish nets outside set a rural scene which endures in the face of mushrooming housing and industrial estates.

Ang Sila and Saam Muk

Beyond the uninteresting provincial capital of **Chon Buri** is the tiny fishing village of **Ang Sila**, known for its locally made stone mortars and pestles. The place makes no concession to the visitor, something sufficiently rare as to rank almost as a tourist attraction in itself. The seafood restaurant next to the fish pier can be recommended.

After Ang Sila the road passes oyster farms and follows the coast for about 5km (3 miles) to reach the tiny fishing village of **Saam Muk**. On the outskirts is **Thamma Nava**, a centre for vegetarian nuns and others seeking a spiritual retreat, while a grander sight is the revered temple of **Sala Jao Mae Saam Muk**. Backing onto the limestone cliffs and overlooking Saam Muk's harbour, the temple is unmistakably Chinese, an intricate

DON'T MISS

* **Pattaya**: Thailand's international playground – see it to believe it.
*** **Golf**: Several top courses around Pattaya.
*** **Ko Chang**: Pristine tropical island resort.
** **Ko Samet**: Popular island retreat.
* **Chanthaburi**: Gem mines and markets.

Crocodile farm at Samut Prakan near the mouth of the Chao Phraya river.

and colourful complex of galleries, terraces, glass-fronted shrines and Oriental baroque sculpture all dominated by a huge statue of **Kuan Im**, goddess of Mercy.

Directly opposite Sala Jao Mae Saam Muk are Wang Muk and Thip Pramong restaurants. Both serve excellent crab and other seafood dishes in unpretentious surroundings.

Around the corner and up the hill from Saam Muk is **Monkey Mountain**, a hilltop inhabited by a troop of mischievous monkeys. This is also a vantage point for panoramic sea views. From here, the road continues downhill to reach Bang Saen.

Bang Saen

Located 96km (60 miles) southeast of Bangkok, Bang Saen is a beach resort that predates the tourism boom and retains local popularity. Although hordes of city-dwellers descend at the weekends, a tranquil air prevails during the week, when the 2km (1-mile) grey-sand beach and **Ocean World** water amusement park are near deserted. Worth visiting is the small aquarium attached to the **Institute of Marine Science** (Tue–Sun 08:30–16:00), with fish tanks, two dolphins and a marine science museum.

Ko Si Chang

About 15km (9 miles) further down the coast from Bang Saen is **Si Racha**, where ferries ply the 12km (7½ miles)

GREEN RETREAT

As a change from the beach, **Khao Khieo Open Zoo** provides a pleasant trip into the countryside. About a 40min drive inland from Bang Saen, Khao Khieo covers 486ha (1200 acres) and contains a small collection of animals enclosed in spacious surroundings, and a large aviary. As a zoo it is unexceptional but the quiet, hilly setting and woodland scenery are most attractive. Open daily 07:00–18:00.

GOLFING BREAKS

A 40min drive from the beach leads into some wonderful golfing country. Among the top courses are **Bang Phra**, tel (038) 321–332; **Panya Resort**, tel (038) 322–370; **Siam Country Club**, tel (038) 280–2532; and **Rayong Green Valley Country Club**, tel (038) 603–000. Greens are usually crowded at weekends but fairly quiet during the week.

to Ko Si Chang (first boat 07:00, last return 15:00). This sizeable inhabited island offers rugged scenery and a wonderful sense of escape, as well as a few intriguing sights, including a Chinese temple and the ruins of a summer palace built by King Rama V. Bungalow accommodation is available.

PATTAYA

Facing a wide bay and a long sweep of not very special beach 145km (90 miles) southeast of Bangkok, Pattaya has over the past three decades been groomed for the vacationer seeking sun, sea, sand and sex. What was once a quiet fishing village became first a rest and recuperation centre for US forces during the Vietnam War, and then an international beach-resort playground. Today, Pattaya is bloated by success and, with full city status, suffers the headaches of unbridled development. Water pollution is a serious problem and the resort is further marred by rampant prostitution, both male and female. But, despite it all, Pattaya's all-out effort to provide the most and the best of everything a beach destination should have, and more besides, still has a certain attraction for those who like their resorts brash, bold and bawdy with a dizzying kaleidoscope of activities to choose from.

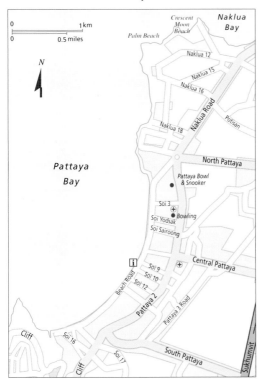

Expanded in all directions from its original core, the resort is centred on the

4km (2¹/₂ mile) **Pattaya Beach**, crowded, cluttered and largely polluted. **Pattaya Beach Road** runs along the shore and is paralleled a little way inland by **Pattaya 2 Road**. Both roads and their numerous linking short lanes (*sois*) are packed with a jumble of hotels, guesthouses, restaurants, fast-food outlets, shops and department stores.

The northern end of the bay is marginally quieter and more upmarket, while in the south is '**The Strip'**, the original fishing village, now a raunchy conglomeration of open-air bars, restaurants, neon-lit go-go bars and shops. Around the southern headland lies **Jomtien Beach**, a better stretch of sand than Pattaya in spite of looming highrise condos.

The brash modern beach resort of Pattaya has a colourful appeal to fun-seeking holidaymakers.

Sports and Entertainment

When it comes to recreational pursuits, Pattaya is unrivalled and the number of sporting options is staggering. In addition to a huge variety of watersports, on-land activities include **archery** (at Nong Nooch Village, tel 429–372); **badminton** (Pattaya Badminton Courts, Soi 17, tel 429–532); **bowling** (best at Pattaya Bowl, Pattaya 2 Road, tel 429–466); **go-karting** (Pattaya Kart Speedway, tel 423–062); **tennis** (at most main hotels); **rifle and pistol shooting** (Tiffany's, Pattaya 2 Road, tel 429–642); and **snooker** (Pattaya Bowl, Pattaya 2 Road, tel 429–466). There are also occasional weekend motor-racing meets at Bira International Circuit at km 14 on Highway 36 (about 15km/9 miles from Pattaya).

Nightlife attractions range from a metropolitan mix of restaurants to shopping (souvenirs, tailoring, gems and jewellery), go-go bars, cocktail lounges, discos and

WATERSPORTS

Watersports can be practised everywhere in Pattaya, but windsurfing, waterskiing, jet-skiing, parasailing and sailing (mainly Hobie Cats and Prindles) are best at Jomtien. Facilities for snorkelling and scuba diving are plentiful and Pattaya has several dive shops (one recommendation is Seafari Sports Centre at Royal Garden Resort, tel 428–126). For game fishing contact Pattaya Game Fishing Club at Jenny's Hotel, tel 429–645. Yacht charters are operated by Sundowner Sailing Service, tel 423–686, ext 2050.

Traditional Thai boxing takes place at Nong Nooch Cultural Village, Pattaya.

Pattaya's renowned transvestite cabarets – the latter at Tiffany's (tel 421–700) and Alcazar (tel 418–746), both on Pattaya 2 Road.

Among excursion possibilities is **Nong Nooch Cultural Village** (tel 429–321), a privately run country resort 15min by car from Pattaya, with restaurants, mini zoo, landscaped gardens, orchid nursery, performing elephants and daily cultural shows at 10:00 and 15:00. Alternatively, **Mini Siam**, located near Pattaya Klang, offers a collection of famous monuments reproduced on a 1:25 scale. Boat trips to **Ko Larn** and other offshore islands are also available; travel agents organize day excursions to the most popular.

RAYONG

The coastal province of Rayong has a number of good beaches which provide a quieter and much less developed alternative to Pattaya.

The eastern coastline forms a right-angle corner at Sattahip, 30km (20 miles) south of Pattaya, and Rayong's beaches run roughly west to east. A bypass road at Chon Buri cuts off the corner and makes travel time from Bangkok about 2^{1}/2hr.

For travellers interested in taking the coast road beyond Pattaya, one or two places of interest offer themselves. **Wat Yansangworararam**, off to the right some 3km (2 miles) before Nong Nooch Cultural Village, is a good example of modern Thai temple architecture. The extensive grounds are landscaped, while six pavilions in different national styles on the banks of an artificial lake provide additional focal points.

Bang Saray, 15km (9 miles) south of Pattaya and about 4km (2^{1}/2 miles) beyond Wat Yansangworararam,

---

KO SAMET

Best of Rayong's attractions is Ko Samet, a pretty little island noted for its sandy beaches, secluded coves and coral reefs situated some 6km (4 miles) off the coast from Ban Phe. It has long been popular with budget travellers and there is plenty of cheap bungalow accommodation, although the island is officially designated as a national park and development remains controversial.

is a centre for deep-sea sport fishing. It is also renowned for its fine seafood restaurant, Ruantalay, which is set on its own pier and serves excellent, inexpensive food.

Just before the border between Chon Buri and Rayong provinces is **Samae San**, lying on the point of the headland 10km (6 miles) past Sattahip and another 10km (6 miles) off the main road. Although far from picturesque, it is none the less an authentic fishing village with the attraction of three islands close to shore which can be explored by hiring a boat at the fish pier.

The town of Rayong (210 km / 130 miles from Bangkok) is itself unexceptional and the main resort area runs from the fishing village of **Ban Phe** (17 km / 10 miles from town) to **Mae Pim headland** (closest town is **Klaeng**), a distance of about 25km (15 miles). This stretch is virtually all beach, beginning with **Ban Kon Ao**, west of Ban Phe, and **Hat Mae Ram Phung**, extending for several kilometres on the eastern side. Bungalow-style accommodation predominates, although resort luxury is offered by Rayong Resort, situated on its own private headland west of Ban Phe, and Palmeraie Beach Hotel, located some 20km (12 miles) east of Ban Phe, not far from **Sunthorn Phu Monument** (a memorial park to Thailand's greatest poet).

KO CHANG

With provincial capitals situated 330km (200 miles) and 400km (250 miles) from Bangkok respectively, Thailand's two easternmost provinces of **Chanthaburi** and **Trat** are famous for fruit and gems, although most of the gem fields are worked out and most stones now come from neighbouring Cambodia. There is still an active gem market in **Chanthaburi town**, but the bigger attraction lies next door in Trat province, where the island of Ko Chang affords an idyllic retreat.

Situated 8km (5 miles) off the coast of Trat and measuring 30km (18 miles) long and 8km (5 miles) across at its widest point, Ko Chang is Thailand's second largest island, yet it has only a sparse population (mostly fishermen), no towns and scarcely any road. It is the principal

Tourist bungalows offer an idyllic retreat among the palm trees of Ko Chang.

isle in the 52-island archipelago which forms **Mu Ko Chang Marine National Park**, established as a nature preserve in 1982. Ko Chang itself has a mountainous interior which accounts for the name, 'Elephant Island'; a fanciful notion has it that from a distance the mountain ridges look like the backs of several elephants. The rugged interior, peaking at 744m (2441ft), remains roughly 70% virgin rainforest, and the dense, lush greenery contrasts with a coastline characterized by small bays and exceptionally fine white sandy beaches. The best spots are on the western side of the island, notably, from north to south, at **Ao Khlong Son**, **Hat Sai Khao**, **Hat Khlong Phrao** and **Ao Kai Bae**.

Other principal islands in the archipelago are **Ko Kut**, **Ko Mak** and **Ko Kradat**. All of these main islands offer some bungalow-style accommodation – more ambitious projects are in the pipeline – but at present Ko Chang itself has the only true first-class hotel, Ko Chang Resort.

There is little in the way of organized activity on Ko Chang, but that is what a visit is all about – a blissful escape into a world where the sky is bluer and the colours of nature more vivid. There are a couple of waterfalls to visit, such as **Klong Plu Ko** close by Ko Chang Resort, and most bungalows hire motorbikes for negotiating the island's few rudimentary roads. But the island's character is changing as more facilities are added; while Ko Chang's best season is from Nov–May, the time to visit is *now* – in a few years' time these lovely islands will be just another beach resort.

CHANTHABURI TOWN

The Church of the Immaculate Conception in Chanthaburi town is Thailand's largest cathedral. The French-style building dates from 1906, although a chapel was first erected in the early 18th century. Vietnamese refugees account for much of Chanthaburi's sizeable Christian population.

East Coast at a Glance

GETTING THERE

Bang Saen: Bang Saen is 1–1¹/₂hr by car from Bangkok. Buses go throughout the day from Bangkok.

Pattaya: Buses depart every 30min 06:00–21:00 from Bangkok. Diamond Coach Company runs thrice-daily each-way deluxe coach services with hotel pick-ups.

Rayong: Hourly buses (about 2 1/2hr) from Bangkok to Rayong town, Ban Phe or Klaeng.

Ko Chang: Air-conditioned (blue) buses (5–6hr) from Bangkok to Trat bus station every 2hr 07:00–23:00. Thence take *songthaew* (15min) to Laem Ngop pier, from which boats to Ko Chang go at various times of day, different ferries to different parts of the island (to near side c1hr, to western shore c2hr). Ko Chang Resort runs own boat transfers.

GETTING AROUND

Pattaya: *Songthaews* ply Beach Road and Pattaya 2 Road. Jeeps and motorbikes are readily hired. Vehicles are usually uninsured and you are liable for any damage or injury; best to hire from a proper shop or travel agent rather than a kerbside rank.

WHERE TO STAY

Bang Saen
Bangsaen Villa Resort, 140/16 Mu 14, tel (038) 381–772 Best option, good atmosphere.

SS Bangsaen Beach Hotel, 245/52 Mu 13, Tambon **Saensuk**, tel (038) 381–670, fax (038) 381–963 Comfortable but rather characterless.

Pattaya
Royal Cliff Beach Resort, Cliff Road, South Pattaya, tel (038) 421–421, fax (038) 428–511 Long-established, pleasantly isolated on headland south of Pattaya with private beach.

Dusit Resort, 240/2 Beach Road, tel (038) 425–611, fax (038) 428–239; BKK Res. tel 236–0450 Superb amenities; secluded location at north end of bay.

Siam Bayshore, Beach Road, tel (038) 428–678 Close to 'The Strip', but well set back in own grounds.

Royal Garden Resort, Beach Road, tel (038) 428–126 Good value; central location.

Palm Garden, 485 Pattaya 2 Road, tel (038) 429–099 Quiet and an excellent choice on all counts.

Rayong
Palmeraie Beach Hotel, 177 Moo 1 Ban Pae-Mae Pim Road, Chark Pong, Klaeng, BKK Res. tel 213–1162, fax

213–1163 Beachfront location and fine facilities.

Rayong Resort, Laem Tarn, Ban Phe, tel (038) 651000, fax (66038) 651007, BKK Res. tel 255–2391 Upmarket and set on own headland.

Ko Chang
Ko Chang Resort, Khlong Phrao beach, BKK Res. tel 277–5256, fax 277–0975 Air-conditioned beach bungalows, best on the island.

Sun Sai Bungalows, White Sand Beach, BKK Res. tel 411–3605 Good beach bungalows.

WHERE TO EAT

Bang Saen: **Seaview**, by Bangsaen Beach Resort, good for seafood. **Coconut Grove**, by Saensook Resort, offers Thai, Chinese seafood, European dishes; inexpensive. **Pattaya**: Dolf Riks offers good European/Indonesian food (*rijsttafel* a house speciality). **PIC Kitchen**, off Beach Road: traditional Thai food/ setting. **Ruenthai**, Pattaya 2 Road: Thai food with cultural show. Nang Nual, Beach Road: good choice for fresh seafood.

PATTAYA	J	F	M	A	M	J	J	A	S	O	N	D
AVERAGE TEMP. °F	79	81	83	85	84	84	83	83	81	81	80	76
AVERAGE TEMP. °C	26	27	28	29	29	29	28	28	28	27	26	25
Hours of Sun Daily	8	8	8	7	6	4	5	5	5	5	6	8
RAINFALL in	1	1	2	3	7	3	3	4	8	10	5	1
RAINFALL mm	19	14	52	67	177	79	77	90	202	249	134	4
Days of Rainfall	1	3	4	6	12	11	11	12	17	18	9	1

7
The South

Southern Thailand occupies the **Kra Peninsula**, a narrow strip of land running more than 1200km (750 miles) from just below Bangkok to the Malaysian border. In spite of a distinct history, a culture coloured by a strong Muslim influence and a number of large, modern towns, the region is best known for its beaches and islands. For practical purposes, we shall divide the South into three main areas: the **Gulf Coast**, the **Andaman Coast** and the **Deep South**.

Extending down the eastern shores of the peninsula, the Gulf Coast resorts begin with **Cha-am** and **Hua Hin**, taking in the nearby historic town of **Phetchaburi**, and continue through **Chumphon** to conclude with popular **Ko Samui**, off the coast of Surat Thani province.

The Andaman coast, on the western side of the peninsula, takes in **Phuket island**, Thailand's top beach resort, as well as the **Phi Phi islands**, the **Similan islands** (a first-class dive spot), **Phang Nga Bay** and **Krabi**, the latter distinguished by magnificent coastal scenery.

The Deep South has less spectacular beaches, a more traditional southern culture and less developed scenery. The main resort is unassuming **Songkhla**, supported by the neighbouring large town of **Hat Yai**.

In addition to regular bus services from Bangkok to all points south, Hua Hin, Chumphon and Surat Thani are on the southern rail link, while Phuket, Ko Samui, Surat Thani and Hat Yai are served by scheduled flights. Phuket is further served by flights from Hong Kong, Malaysia, Singapore and other overseas locations.

CLIMATE

Ko Samui island is affected by the northeast monsoon and thus the rains come in Oct–Jan. Elsewhere the usual pattern prevails, although the rainy season is longer and wetter on the Andaman coast, and the annual temperature range is less pronounced. Phuket's high season is Nov–Feb.

Opposite: *Scenic coves and magnificent beaches on the western shore of Phuket.*

DON'T MISS

** **Phetchaburi**: Historic town.
** **Hua Hin**: Thailand's oldest beach resort.
*** **Phuket**: Tropical island resort.
*** **Phang Nga Bay**: Offers a haunting seascape.
*** **Krabi**: Spectacular resort setting.
*** **Ko Samui**: Island escape in the Gulf.
* **Songkhla**: Quiet seaside town.

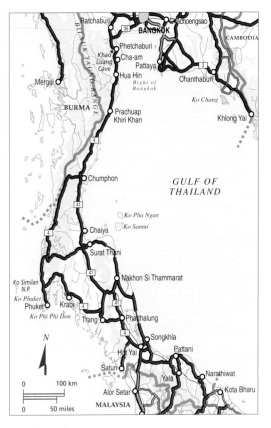

THE GULF COAST
Phetchaburi **

Travelling south from Bangkok by road or rail, Phetchaburi is the first town of note, although most travellers pass it by in their hurry to get to the beach resorts beyond. This is a pity as the town, located 126km (78 miles) south of Bangkok on the banks of the Phet Buri river, offers a surprising wealth of historical and architectural sights.

An established settlement in the pre-Thai Khmer period, Phetchaburi later developed as an important artistic centre during the Ayutthaya era. Regal status was bestowed in the mid-19th century when King Mongkut, Rama IV, built **Phra Nakhon Khiri (Khao Wang)** on the hill outside town, although after the monarch's death in 1868 the palace fell into disuse and Phetchaburi sank into obscurity. With a mostly unattractive modern overlay, the town today looks scruffy and lacks good hotels. But it is not necessary to stay overnight; half a day's sightseeing is sufficient before continuing on to the beach resorts less than an hour's drive away.

The town of Phetchaburi is undistinguished but it is a good stopping-point for exploring the nearby wealth of historical and archaeological sites.

Phra Nakhon Khiri (Khao Wang) *

Dominating Phetchaburi's northern outskirts, this hilltop palace can be reached by cable car or by a winding pathway edged with frangipani.

The restored palace buildings, including an astronomical observatory, are interesting for their blend of Thai and Western influences – a stylistic trend further reflected in furniture and other domestic artefacts exhibited in a small museum. Possibly more impressive are the superlative views of the town and of the surrounding countryside.

Khao Luang Cave Shrine *

Some 3km (2 miles) from Khao Wang is the cave shrine of Khao Luang. A steep staircase leads down to the cavern's entrance and an opening in the roof allows the sunlight to illuminate the huge central chamber, which enshrines numerous Buddha statues, the principal one being **Luang Poh Tham Luang**, a large seated image dating from King Mongkut's reign.

Wat Mahathat's soaring prang *towers above the centre of Phetchaburi.*

Wat Yai Suwannaram ★★★

In town, Wat Yai Suwannaram dates from the 17th century, having been built during the reign of Rama V, and presents a splendid collection of finely proportioned and richly adorned buildings which make it one of the most beautiful temples in Thailand. Additional interest lies in the well preserved mural paintings covering the interior walls of the temple's main hall.

Wat Ko Keo Suttharam ★★★

This is another of Phetchaburi's venerable temples, and is similarly important for its murals. Dated to 1734, the paintings display a different inspiration to those of Wat Yai Suwannaram and, despite a more restricted range of colours, are striking in their detail and unusual composition.

Wat Mahathat ★★★

The central spire of Wat Mahathat is an unmistakable Phetchaburi landmark. This towering *prang* rises from the middle of a cloister lined with Buddha images (the temple is home to 198 Buddha statues in all), and is surrounded by smaller *prangs*, each with a small chapel. Inside the temple's main hall are three large presiding Buddhas, each on a different level, with the tallest one being characterized by its Ayutthaya style of statuary. The interior walls are covered with murals which, although not as good as those at Wat Yai Suwannaram and at Wat Ko Keo Suttharam, are worthy of note. Wat Mahathat is a popular local focal point and the daily activity it attracts is fascinating to observe.

Wat Kamphaeng Laeng ★

The ruins of this Khmer-period temple are not as impressive as those found in Northeast Thailand. Contained within partially surviving original walls are a large central *prang*, three smaller towers of similar design in various stages of collapse, and the remains of a *gopura* (ornamental covered gateway). This is the oldest site in Phetchaburi, dating from the 13th century.

KHAO SAM ROI YOT

South of Hua Hin and accessible by road, the National Park of Khao Sam Roi Yot ('Mountain of 300 Peaks') is worth a detour. Its headquarters are 38km (23 miles) from Pranburi town, itself 25km (15 miles) from Hua Hin. Covering an area of some 100 sq km (40 sq miles), the park comprises a series of towering limestone outcrops, and the habitat of cliffs, marshes, mangroves, coves and caves is home to a variety of fauna, especially birds, of which 885 species have been sighted. Khao Sam Roi Yot is notable also for its superb coastal panoramas, and near the park office a signposted path leads up to a vantage point which affords breathtaking views.

Cha-am and Hua Hin **

The beach destinations of Cha-am and Hua Hin respectively lie 40km (25 miles) and 67km (41 miles) south of Phetchaburi. Characterized by a long, casuarina-fringed beach, Cha-am is the smaller of the two resorts. Uncrowded during the week, it teems at weekends when a typical Thai holiday atmosphere prevails.

Hua Hin is larger and more upmarket. It similarly has a long uncluttered beach which, separated at one end from a still-active fishing village by a rocky headland, curves gently for some 3km (2 miles) to its southern point, where a Buddhist temple clings to the cliffs. Beyond lies another beach, **Hat Khao Tao**, pine-fringed and more secluded.

The main attraction of both Cha-am and Hua Hin is the opportunity both offer for simply lazing by the beach. For the more energetic, a variety of watersports can be enjoyed, and Hua Hin also boasts a very picturesque golf course, but neither resort attempts to imitate Pattaya's frenzied activity. Hua Hin, in particular, preserves much of its traditional Thai identity, most obviously around the little fishing port (where there are a couple of good local seafood restaurants) and at the night market.

Chumphon **

Briefly and disastrously in the news in 1989 when it was hit by a typhoon (a rare occurrence in Thailand),

OLDEST RESORT

Hua Hin is Thailand's oldest beach resort, rising to prominence in the 1920s when it became a popular royal and aristocratic hot-season retreat. Today, the past can be glimpsed at the **Hotel Sofitel Central**, the renovated incarnation of the old colonial-style Railway Hotel.

The historic railway station at Hua Hin.

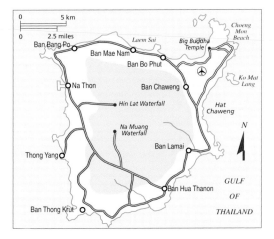

Chumphon otherwise remains obscure. However, the province, situated 500km (310 miles) south of Bangkok, has a 220km (137-mile) coastline with beaches well away from the shadow of condos and highrise construction cranes. In addition, there are excellent conditions for snorkelling and scuba diving, with the first really worthwhile coral reefs in the upper part of the Gulf.

Chumphon provincial capital has little to recommend it other than its southern character. There is a largish night market with an ethnic ambience and a number of food stalls worth browsing around. Otherwise the main attraction is the beaches north and south of the town.

KO SAMUI

Top spot on the Gulf Coast is Ko Samui, Thailand's third largest island, located some 650km (400 miles) south of Bangkok and 35km (21 miles) off the coast of Surat Thani. The island covers an area of about 280 sq km (108 sq miles), and measures 21km (13 miles) at its widest point and 25km (15 miles) in maximum length.

A mountain ridge runs east to west and most of the hinterland comprises forested hills and coconut plantations, while the coast is dotted with palm-fringed beaches and quiet coves.

CHUMPHON'S BEACHES

Top of the list is **Ao Thung Wua Laen**, a beautiful long palm-fringed stretch of sand about 12km (7 miles) north of Chumphon town. Accommodation here is provided by the Chumphon Cabana Resort, complete with dive shop and scuba school. (Note: the best dive spot, say the experts, is Ko Tao, 'Turtle Island', about 50 km/30 miles from Chumphon – 4 or 5hr by boat.)

South of Chumphon town are **Pharadon Phap** and **Sai Ree** beaches. Neither is quite as good as Ao Thung Wua Laen, but they are still attractive, and the islands are closer to shore here.

With its picture-postcard beauty, Samui is everyone's dream of a tropical island. Until recently, actually living that dream was limited mostly to backpackers, but now upmarket travellers are attracted by the ease of air access and the availability of deluxe resort hotels. Despite this, beach bungalows and a youthful, casual atmosphere still predominate.

Travellers arriving by air land at **Samui airport** in the northeast corner of the island, close to the action, while the ferries from Surat Thani dock on the less-developed western shore, either at **Na Thon**, the main town, or slightly further south. A 59km (36-mile) ringroad provides ready access to all points.

The island's two major accommodation beaches are Chaweng and Lamai, both on the east coast. Stretching for 6km (4 miles) and fringed with palms, **Chaweng** is

> ### LUCKY SHRINE
>
> Chumphon's only noted landmark is a shrine at the northern end of Pharadon Phap Beach that honours Prince Chumphon, 'Father of the Thai Navy'. Amazingly, this revered spot was totally undamaged when Typhoon Gay struck in 1989, a lucky escape which local belief says was due to the winds being soothed by the spirit of Prince Chumphon.

Ko Samui is the tropical island you have seen in your dreams.

Boathouse-style holiday dwellings on Ko Samui.

the more popular and offers a remarkable range of accommodation and other facilities. **Lamai**, a few kilometres to the south, is also a pretty beach but its development has been more downmarket.

The north side of the island is very quiet and mostly unspoilt, the only major development being at **Mae Nam Beach**, the site of the deluxe Santiburi resort. Directly east of Mae Nam, **Bo Phut** is also peaceful, though less beautiful, while further eastward is **Big Buddha Beach**, a small bay with views of two offshore islands, one topped by a large seated Buddha. On Samui's northeastern tip is the attractive **Choeng Mon Beach**.

The western and southern coasts lack the dramatic beauty of the north and eastern shores, but reward exploration (easiest by hired motorbike) with a number of quiet and pleasantly isolated coves and bays.

Away from the beaches, sights include two waterfalls, **Hin Lat**, close to Na Thon, and the rather more impressive **Na Muang Waterfall**, about 10km (6 miles) southeast of town.

ISLAND EXCURSIONS

Boats can be hired for trips to **Ko Pha Ngan**, the nearest and largest island next to Samui. Beaches and scenery are as good as on Samui but the island is even quieter and less developed.

A full-day excursion can be made to **Ang Thong Marine Park**, a group of 40 islands situated 30km (20 miles) northwest of Samui with superb limestone formations, caves, lagoons and stunning beaches. Organized daily tours to Ang Thong are available from travel agents in Na Thon.

Surat Thani and Chaiya *

On the mainland, the main hopping-off point for Samui is Surat Thani, a fishing and shipbuilding centre. A casual stroll around town or a canal tour on the Tapi river offers glimpses of typical southern life.

Of more specific interest is Chaiya, about a 45min drive north of Surat Thani. It has historical importance as one possible site of the capital of the ancient Sriwijaya kingdom, although little obvious evidence remains. Chaiya's main sight is **Wat Phra Boromathat Chaiya**, a highly revered temple with a *chedi* believed to be more than 1000 years old and thus one of the few surviving examples of Sriwijayan architecture. **Wat Wieng Sa**, **Wat Long** and **Wat Kaeo** are also worth visiting. A few kilometres outside Chaiya is **Wat Suan Mokkha**, a well known Buddhist meditation centre for both Thais and foreigners set amid a peaceful natural park.

Nakhon Si Thammarat **

Located 140km (87 miles) south of Surat Thani, Nakhon Si Thammarat is the South's second largest city and one of the oldest settlements in the country. It was a major centre during the Sriwijaya period, and although something of a backwater today, the town manages to exude an air of historical importance. Culturally, Nakhon Si Thammarat is known for **manora** dance drama, buffalo-hide shadow puppets and nielloware, a silver and black alloy used in jewellery and ornaments. The town's foremost sight is **Wat Mahathat** (open daily 08:30–16:30),

Dramatic limestone formations rise from the sea at Ang Thong.

which possibly dates from AD757. The temple complex, dominated by a 77m (253ft) *chedi*, comprises several *viharns* of considerable interest. Directly south of Wat Phra Mahathat is **Phra Viharn Luang**, a much-restored masterpiece of Ayutthaya architectural style with a roof raised on inward-leaning pillars. Further south, the **National Museum** (Wed–Sun 09:00–16:00) houses a small but worthwhile collection of antiquities from the region.

THE ANDAMAN COAST
Ranong *
First of the Andaman Coast provinces is Ranong, also distinguished as Thailand's wettest and least populated province. Without rail or air links, Ranong is a trifle cut off, but it can be a refreshing stop for anyone travelling south by road. The provincial capital has a certain charm in its surviving old-style Sino-Portuguese architecture, while its atmosphere and market especially are coloured by the proximity of the Burmese border at **Victoria Point**. About 2km (1¹/₂ mile) east of Ranong town, at **Wat Tapotharam**, there are natural hot springs. Providing first-class hotel and spa facilities is the Jansom Thara Hotel, where water naturally heated to 65°C (149°F) is piped to a swimming pool and jacuzzi.

Mu Ko Surin National Park ***
This collection of five lovely islands with long white sandy beaches and coral reefs (superb conditions for

A trading boat from Victoria Point, on the Burmese border, approach-es Ranong.

snorkelling) lies in adjoining **Phang Nga Province**, but can be reached on day trips arranged by the Jansom Thara Hotel on Fridays and weekends. Alternatively, local boats leave from **Ban Hin Lad**, near the town of **Khura Buri** in Phang Nga Province. The boat journey from the mainland takes about 3–4hr. The National Park headquarters and bungalow accommodation are located on **Surin Nua** island.

Laem Son National Park *
Some 60km (37 miles) south of Ranong, Laem Son National Park is a coastal area offering beaches, mangrove swamps, coral reefs and 20 offshore islands.

PHUKET
Thailand's largest island (albeit linked to the mainland by a causeway), Phuket is a province in itself and the country's premier beach destination some 900km (560 miles) south of Bangkok. From being a backpackers' mecca in the 1970s, the island has rocketed to tourism stardom and today hosts annually more than $1^1/_2$ million visitors who flock to the island's superb beaches and fine resort hotels. The rapid growth of the travel industry has had some negative impact (**Patong Beach**, for example, is now overbuilt), but, at 48km (30 miles) long by 21km (13 miles) wide, the island can sustain considerable development without sacrificing essential characteristics.

No stranger to either fame or wealth, Phuket has long

Paddy fields in southern Thailand. Rice, the country's primary crop, thrives in the humid climate.

Phuket's beautiful white beaches are set against a backdrop of lush tropical vegetation.

PHUKET SPORTS

A wide choice of watersports is available from the more developed beaches, such as Patong and Karon. In particular Phuket is a major centre for scuba diving and yacht charters (with or without crew). Several reliable dive shops are located at Patong, Karon and in town. Among yacht charterers are Yacht Charter Company, tel (076) 216–556; Travel Company, tel (076) 321–292; Asia Voyages, tel (076) 216–137; and Marinasia, tel (076) 213–405.

For a break away from the beach, Phuket offers superb international-standard golf courses at the following locations: Phuket Country Club, tel (076) 213–388; Blue Canyon Country Club, tel (076) 327–440; Banyan Tree Club, tel (076) 324–350.

been on the map – literally, as Claudius Ptolemy included on his 2nd-century map of Southeast Asia an unnamed projection that is probably Phuket. Certainly the island was known to early Arab and Indian seafarers and later, in the 16th and 17th centuries, to various Western explorers and traders. Then called **Junkceylon**, the island was renowned for its natural harbours, its tin deposits and its pirates.

In the 18th century, Captain Francis Light hesitated

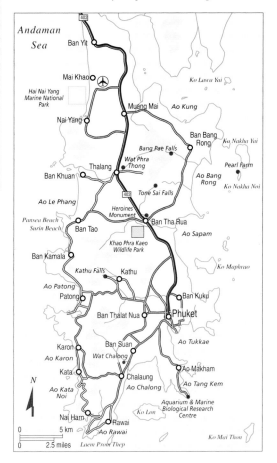

whether to claim Phuket or the Malay island of Penang for the British. He eventually plumped for the latter, thus saving Phuket from a colonial fate.

Quick to follow up on what the British had ignored were the Burmese, who first attacked the island in 1785. They met greater resistance than they bargained for in the form of two sisters, Chan and Muk, who broke the Burmese siege of the island. (The two women are honoured today in a statue standing at one of the island's road intersections.)

After a further unsuccessful Burmese invasion, the 19th century brought peace and prosperity when tin mining boomed following a huge influx of Chinese immigrants. In the 20th century, rubber and now tourism have replaced tin as the source of wealth, maintaining Phuket's standing as Thailand's richest province.

Culturally, the island has over the centuries been a melting pot, and today it offers an intriguing mix of Thai, Chinese and Muslim traditions, with differences most readily seen in the juxtaposition of Thai Buddhist temples, garish Chinese temples and the minarets of mosques. Lifestyles vary from those of the rural Thai and the Muslim fishing communities to the urban pursuits of the Chinese immigrants.

For the most part, Phuket remains tranquil and easygoing. The island's interior is one of forested hills and valleys chequered with rubber, coconut and pineapple plantations. The land drops to a rugged coastline on the east side, while the gently sloping western shore harbours a succession of magnificent beaches. Major beaches are described below, from north to south.

Patong, once a small fishing village, is now Phuket's major centre for tourism.

• **Mai Khao and Nai Yang**: These two beaches form Phuket's longest strand at some 16km (10 miles). Here giant sea turtles struggle ashore between November and January to lay their eggs.

• **Ban Tao**: An 8km (5-mile) beach where four international-standard resorts all blend surprisingly well into the huge landscape site.

• **Pansea and Surin**: These two scenic coves offer very picturesque settings, although dangerous undercurrents

VEGETARIAN FESTIVAL

The most dramatic example of Chinese influence on Phuket is the Vegetarian Festival held in Oct. This nine-day religious rite, celebrated at the island's five major Chinese temples, is essentially an act of purification and is most spectacularly celebrated by acts of self-mortification. Devotees walk over hot coals, pierce their cheeks with skewers, climb knife-blade ladders and submit to similar ordeals without apparent harm.

Fine example of old colo-nial-style architecture in Phuket town.

can make swimming unsafe.

• **Kamala Beach**: This is the location of one of Phuket's few remaining Muslim fishing villages where a tradition-al way of life can still be glimpsed.

• **Patong Beach**: A majestic curve of sand that has caught the developers' eyes in a big way. Hotels, restaurants, shops and beer huts clutter the shore, and extensive watersports and entertainment facilities have been pro-vided at the expense of the natural setting.

• **Karon and Kata**: The next two beaches, the latter divided by a promontory into big and small coves, are quieter and maintain a fine balance between natural and man-made attractions.

• **Nai Harn**: The island's southernmost beach presents a superb sweep of sand facing a delightful bay and backed by a lagoon. There is one deluxe resort hotel but little other development. On the southern tip is **Laem Prom Thep headland**, a noted beauty spot and favourite van-tage point for watching Phuket's spectacular sunsets.

• **Rawai Beach**: Around the point from Nai Harn, this beach is noted for its village of sea gypsies, a once semi-nomadic waterborne people descended from some of the island's earliest inhabitants. The beach is not particularly good for swimming but longtail boats leave from here to offshore islands.

Phuket Town *

In spite of having a couple of first-class hotels, Phuket town acts primarily as a service centre for the beach resorts. Situated in the southwest corner of the island, it has been much developed in recent years and only ves-tiges of its once characteristic Sino-Portuguese shop-house architecture remain – best glimpsed along Yaowarat, Ranong and Phang Nga roads. Worth a visit is **Put Jaw**, Phuket's oldest and largest Chinese temple on Ranong Road. Overlooking the town is **Khao Rang hill** from whose summit are fine panoramic views.

Around Phuket

• **Marine Biological Research Centre**: There is a good

aquarium here with a variety of both ocean and fresh-water fish. Open daily 10:00–16:00.

• **Butterfly Garden and Aquarium**: Landscaped open-air enclosure with thousands of colourful butterflies, plus an excellent tropical aquarium. Open daily 09:00–17:30.

• **Naga Pearl Farm**: This well known commercial pearl farm offers tours and demonstrations of pearl culturing. Located on Naga Noi Island and accessible by boat from Po Bay; contact Naga Pearl Tour and Resort, tel (076) 213–723. Open daily 09:00–15:30.

• **Wat Chalong**: One of Phuket's largest Buddhist tem-ples, Wat Chalong in the south of the island behind Chalong Bay is highly revered for the images of two of its former abbots who possessed legendary healing skills.

• **Wat Phra Thong**: Located in Thalang District, this tem-ple is famous for its gold (now covered with plaster) Buddha image half-buried in the ground. Legend has it that many people have died trying unsuccessfully to unearth the statue.

• **Khao Phra Thaeo National Park**: The last surviving patch of the rainforest that once covered the island. Lush flora plus attractive waterfalls located close to Thalang.

The pearl farm on Naga Noi island offers tours as well as demonstrations of pearl culturing.

Although suffering from commercial exploitation, much of Phi Phi Don is still exquisitely beautiful.

Excursions From Phuket
Phang Nga ★★★

Made famous in the 1970s as a location for the James Bond movie *The Man With the Golden Gun*, the island-studded Phang Nga Bay is the most popular day excursion from Phuket. Belonging to the mainland province north of Phuket, Phang Nga can be reached by bus from Phuket to Phang Nga town and then boat from Tha Don Pier, or directly by boat from Po Bay on the northeast side of Phuket. For the adventurous, there are also sea canoeing tours; contact Sea Canoe Thailand, tel/fax (076) 212–172.

Fringed by mangrove swamps, Phang Nga Bay is given dramatic beauty by scores of limestone karst formations. Thrown up by shifts in the earth's crust some 75 million years ago, these strange rocky islands have over the millennia been eroded into weird and fantastic shapes. Swathed in tangles of creepers and shrubs, some of the outcrops rise sheer from the water, others are humped or jagged; some are little more than rocks, while others have precipitous cliffs large enough to conceal caves and grottoes.

Phi Phi Islands ★★★

Ton Sai Bay on Phi Phi Don is easily accessible by boat from Phuket.

Located 50km (30 miles) east of Phuket, these two small islands of exquisite beauty have long been popular, either as a day excursion from Phuket or as a base for a few days' snorkelling and lazing on the beach. The bigger of the two islands, **Phi Phi Don**, is shaped like a lop-sided butterfly with a thin strand joining the two 'wings'; the left side has high scrub-covered cliffs, while the right-hand span comprises a jungle-clad spine flanked on either side by palm-fringed beaches. On the central strand is **Ao Ton Sai**, where the boats from Phuket dock and where there is, lamentably, an ever-expanding jumble of bungalow accommodation and other facilities. Despite such obvious signs of exploitation, much of the island is still stunning.

The smaller **Phi Phi Le** island is uninhabited and is more rugged, characterized by spectacular sheer cliffs where the edible birds' nests so beloved of Chinese gourmets are harvested. The island needs to be toured by boat for a view of its idyllic bays, hidden coves and other sights such as **Viking Cave**, a splendid grotto with stalactites and ancient wall paintings of sailing ships.

Access to Phi Phi is hugely varied, ranging from converted fishing boats to luxury cruise ships operated by numerous tour companies in Phuket. The main departure point is **Makam Bay**, while access is also possible from Krabi, the mainland province of which the Phi Phi islands are actually a part.

Similan Islands **

Situated 90km (56 miles) northwest of Phuket, the nine Similan islands form a national park. They lack the obvious beauty of the Phi Phi islands, but with crystal-clear water and colourful coral they are arguably Thailand's finest scuba-diving spot. Trips to the Similans are offered by various Phuket tour companies.

KRABI

Located some 800km (500 miles) from Bangkok on the mainland opposite Phuket and south of Phang Nga, Krabi province has perhaps Thailand's most scenic coastline, characterized by karst outcrops which form sheer cliffs on land and islands offshore. The interior is typified by densely wooded hills, palm groves and rubber plantations. The area's beaches are now being developed for tourism, but Krabi remains for the moment a fresher choice than Phuket or Samui.

'Sea gipsy' stilt village in Phang Nga Bay.

Hat Noppharat Thara **

Some 18km (11 miles) northwest of Krabi town, this 2km (1-mile) casuarina-lined beach is part of a national marine park. This pleasant spot is popular with local picnickers but is otherwise little developed.

Ao Nang ***

This is Krabi's main beach, a long sandy strand readily accessible by road. Offshore are numerous islands while

at the southern end of the beach is **Laem Phra Nang**. This enchanting headland can be reached only by boat and offers three stunningly beautiful beaches (**Ao Phra Nang**, the best spot, and **west and east Railae**). Also on the headland are **Phra Nang Cave**, on the beach and housing a shrine to the spirit of Phra Nang, and **'Princess Pool'** high up in the cliffs.

Krabi Town *

The market and wharf in Krabi town, an unpretentious huddle at the mouth of the Krabi river, are worth strolling around for their local colour. **Khanab Nam Mount**, an interesting rock formation in the river and accessible in a few minutes by boat, is also an attraction.

Shell Cemetery *

Much vaunted in Krabi's promotional literature is the Shell Cemetery (Su San Hoi), a beach of fossilized layers of limestone and shells formed 75 million years ago. It is apparently a rare phenomenon, although visually it is no more exciting than the broken concrete slabs of a seaside promenade.

Krabi province boasts some of the most spectacular stretches of coastline in all Thailand.

Wat Tham Sua ★★★

Situated about 7km (4 miles) inland from Krabi town, Tiger Cave Monastery, as the name translates, is a famous forest monastery set in a wooded valley surrounded by high cliffs where monks have meditation shelters in the mouths of caves. The setting is quite extraordinary and most atmospheric.

Tham Bokkhorani National Park

Off the main Krabi–Phang Nga highway some 46km (28 miles) from town, this popular beauty spot is enclosed by limestone cliffs which enhance a fantasy-like setting where the focal point is a large lotus pool fed by a waterfall splashing down from the rocks overhead. Streams flow out from the lagoon and meander through a botanical garden of tropical flowers, trees and shrubs.

THE DEEP SOUTH

The southernmost provinces of **Songkhla**, **Satun**, **Pattani**, **Yala** and **Narathiwat** have nothing to match Phuket, Samui or Krabi in terms of natural beauty and tourism facilities. The region does have its attractions, but they are rewarding only for those who like to explore every corner of the Kingdom, or for visitors travelling overland to or from Malaysia.

Hat Yai and Songkhla ★

Gateway to the Deep South is Hat Yai in Songkhla province. Located 947km (591 miles) from Bangkok, this brash, modern town is a commercial, shopping and entertainment centre with good road, rail and air access but little in the way of charm.

Much more attractive for the visitor is Songkhla, an old and sleepy little coastal resort situated a 30min drive by bus or taxi from Hat Yai. The town boasts two beaches – pleasantly sited **Son Onn Beach** and the 3km (2-mile) pine-fringed stretch of **Samila Beach** – while among cultural sights are **Songkhla National Museum**, the 400-year-old temple of **Wat Matchimawat**, **Wat Chaimongkhom**, where the main pagoda enshrines a

Brightly painted fishing
boats crowd the waterfront
at Pattani.

holy relic of the Lord Buddha, and the 19th-century **Pak Nam Laem Sai For**t.

North of Songkhla town extends the vast expanse of **Songkhla Lake**, Thailand's largest body of inland water. It contains several islands and, near Songkhla, there is **Khu Khut Waterfowl Park**, a sanctuary that supports about 140 bird species.

Satun

On the west coast of the peninsula, Satun province borders the Andaman Sea. Its main attraction is **Tarutao Marine National Park**, located 31km (19 miles) off the coast. A wealth of marine life is to be found around the cluster of 51 islands. On the islands are largely untouched forests which provide a habitat for wild boars, macaques, langurs, mouse deer and numerous bird species. Boats to Tarutao leave from **Pak Bara**, 60km (37 miles) north of Satun town.

Also recommended in Satun is the little-visited **Thale Ban National Park**, where forest-covered hills, a lake and an abundance of wildlife combine to make this a stunningly attractive nature reserve. Basic bungalow accommodation is available.

Pattani

Situated on the Gulf of Thailand, 1055km (656 miles) south of Bangkok, Pattani Province has the twin distinction of fine beaches and a thriving Muslim culture. **Pattani Central Mosque**, located on the outskirts of the provincial capital, is Thailand's largest mosque and a focal point for Thai Muslims. **Kruesae Mosque**, 7km (4 miles) from Pattani town, was founded in the late 16th century and, according to legend, was never finished owing to the curse of the Goddess Lim Ko Niao, recognized today in an annual festival celebrated during the third lunar month.

Notable among mostly deserted beaches are pine-fringed **Ratchadapisek Beach**, west of Pattani town, **Talo Kapo Beach**, to the east, and **Khae Khae** in Panarae district on the way to Narathiwat.

Yala

Thailand's southernmost province, Yala is an area of mountains and forests.

The province is most famous for its large ancient statue of the reclining Buddha, enshrined in a cave at **Wat Khuhaphimuk**, 8km (5 miles) from town. Dating from the 8th century (Sriwijaya period), this image is considered one of the three most important monuments of the South.

Narathiwat

Apart from the somewhat bawdy frontier border town of **Sungei Golok**, Narathiwat province boasts one of the South's most beautiful beaches, a 2km (1-mile) stretch of white sand just outside the provincial capital. Cultural attractions include the 24m (79ft) golden seated Buddha image of **Mingmongkhon Thaksin**, **Thaksin Ratcha Nivet Palace** and the old Buddhist temple of **Wat Chonthala Singhe**.

NARATHIWAT VILLAGE

The charming fishing village of Narathiwat lies 100km (60 miles) to the south of Pattani beyond a string of deserted beaches. Despite the absence of any great monuments or historical sites, the town's pleasing wooden architecture and relaxed atmosphere make it an excellent place to retreat from the more tourist-infested resorts of southern Thailand.

The best time to visit is in Sep, when Narathiwat celebrates the king's temporary residence with colourful parades, local handicraft displays and flotillas of brightly painted *kolae*, traditional Malay fishermen's boats.

The South at a Glance

GETTING THERE

Cha-am and Hua Hin: Buses to Cha-am and Hua Hin (about 4hr) leave Bangkok's Southern Bus Terminal in Thonburi hourly 06:00–18:00. Seven trains (about 4hr) go daily to Hua Hin from Bangkok's Hualampong station. Bangkok Airways operates flights to Hua Hin (25min).

Chumphon: Chumphon is roughly 6hr drive from Bangkok. Several daily buses from Bangkok. Six trains (about 8hr) daily from Hualampong station. THAI flights go from Bangkok to Surat Thani, whence the 120km (75 miles) to Chumphon can be covered by bus.

Samui: Bangkok Airways has several daily flights from Bangkok (70min) but has a poor on-time/cancellation record. THAI flights, trains and buses depart Bangkok for Surat Thani, whence there are ferries from Ban Don Pier (night ferry dep. 23:00; travel time 6hr) and Tha Thong, 5km (3 miles) from town (three daily express boats, travel time 2¹/₂hr). Vehicle ferries (about 1hr) leave from Don Sak, 60km (37 miles) from Surat Thani town. Songserm Travel Centre in Bangkok (tel 281-1463) operates connecting bus and express ferry service.

Phuket: THAI flights (70min) several times daily from Bangkok; Bangkok Airways has daily flights between Ko Samui and Phuket. Also international flights to and from Penang, Kuala Lumpur, Singapore and Hong Kong. Overnight buses from Bangkok take 14-15hr.

Krabi: Only direct transport to Krabi from Bangkok is overnight air-conditioned bus (12hr). From Phuket you can take a taxi or bus for the 2¹/₂hr drive . Songserm Travel Centre in Bangkok operates a combined rail/coach service – overnight train from Bangkok to Surat Thani and then bus.

Hat Yai and Songkhla: THAI has daily flights from Bangkok to Hat Yai. Regular train and bus services.

GETTING AROUND

Cha-am and Hua Hin: *Songthaews* run within city limits; intercity buses run between Cha-am and Hua Hin. Bicycle trishaws available in town.

Samui: *Songthaews* serve the main beaches. Motorbikes can be hired in town and at many other spots.

Phuket: *Songthaews* run between Phuket town and the main beaches. Cars and jeeps can be hired in town. Motorbike rentals are widely available around the island.

Krabi: *Songthaews* between town and Ao Phra Nang beach. Boats to Laem Phra Nang depart from riverfront in Krabi town.

WHERE TO STAY

Cha-am
The Regent Cha-am, Phetkasem Road, tel 471-492 Well established deluxe resort.
White Hotel, 263/32 Ruanchit Road, tel 471-118 Good, reasonable beachfront facilities in heart of town.

Hua Hin
Sofitel Central Hua Hin, 1 Damnoen Kasem Road, tel 512-021; BKK Res. tel 233-0980 Expensive; the old Railway Hotel, splendidly renovated.
Royal Garden Village, 43/1 Phetkasem Road, tel 512-412; BKK Res. tel 476-0022 Deluxe Thai-style complex.
Sailom, 29 Phetkasem Road, tel 511-890; BKK Res. tel 258-0652 Moderately priced with swimming pool

Chumphon
Chumphon Cabana Resort, Thung Wua Laen Beach, tel (077) 501-990; BKK Res. tel 224-1884. Has scuba dive shop.
Sai Ree Lodge, Sai Ree Beach, Pak Nam Chumphon 86120, tel (077) 502-023; fax (077) 502-479; BKK Res. tel 258-6645; fax (077) 259-2232 Comfortable bungalows.
Pharadon Inn, 180/12 Pharadon Road, tel (077) 511-500 Best in town.

Samui
The Imperial Samui, Chaweng Beach, tel (077) 421-390; BKK Res. tel 261-9000, fax 261-9530

The South at a Glance

Excellent deluxe facilities.
The Imperial Tongsai Bay, Choeng Mon Beach, tel (077) 425-015, fax (077) 425-462; BKK Res. tel 261-9000, fax 261-9530
Deluxe Mediterranean-style facilities and great views.
Samui Palm Beach, 174/3 Thaveerat Road, Bophut, tel (077) 425-494; BKK Res. tel 253-8942, fax 253-4005
Excellent mid-range bungalow accommodation; good food.
Laem Set Inn, 110 Moo 2, Hua Thanon, tel (077) 424-393, fax (077) 424-394
Superior rustic bungalows in peaceful setting.

Phuket
Anampuri, Pansea Beach, tel (076) 311-394, fax (076) 311-200; BKK Res. tel 250-0746
Super-deluxe bungalows.
Dusit Laguna, 390 Srisoontron Road, Cherngtalay District, Amphur Talang, tel (076) 311-320/9, fax (076) 311-174; BKK Res. tel 236-0450
Part of Dusit Hotels/Resorts chain.
Pansea, Pansea Bay, tel (076) 311-249
Upmarket bungalow in lovely setting.
Le Meridien Phuket, Karon Beach, tel (076) 321-480, fax (076) 321-479; BKK Res. tel 254-8147
Huge but good.
Phuket Yacht Club, Nai Harn Beach, tel (076) 214-020/6
Super-deluxe and stunning location.
Kata Delight, PO Box 73,

Phuket 83000, tel (076) 212-901/4
Good mid-range resort.
Pearl Hotel, 42 Montri Road, tel (076) 211-044; BKK Res. tel 260-1022
Among oldest/best in town.

Krabi
Dusit Rayavadee, Laem Phra Nang, tel (075) 620-630; BKK Res. tel 236-0450, fax 238-4797
Ultra-deluxe bungalows; part of Dusit Hotels/Resorts chain.
Krabi Resort, 53-7 Pattana Road (Krabi office), tel (075) 611-389; BKK Res. tel 251-8094
On Ao Phra Nang beach.
Phra Nang Inn, Ao Phra Nang, PO Box 25, Krabi, tel (075) 611-389; BKK Res. tel 251-8094
Mid-range wooden beach-front hotel.
Phra Nang Place, Laem Phra Nang, tel (075) 612-172
Good inexpensive bungalows.
Vieng Thong, 155-7 Uttarakij Road, tel (075) 611-188
Cheap; main hotel in town.

Hat Yai and Songkhla
JB Hotel, 99 Chuti-anusorn Road, tel (074) 234-300
Hat Yai's best.
King's, 126-8 Niphat-Uthit 1

Road, tel (074) 243-966
Good budget-priced hotel.
Samila, 1/11 Ratchadamnoen Road, tel (074) 311-310
Best in Songkhla; good value.
Narai, 12/2 Chaikhao Road, tel (074) 311-078
Best of the budget hotels.

WHERE TO EAT

Cha-am /Hua Hin: Outside hotels, best bets are the seafood restaurants by the fishing pier in Hua Hin and foodstalls at the night market.
Chumphon: **Pharadon Phap**, by the beach of the same name, serves excellent and inexpensive seafood.
Samui: Many places to eat but little to distinguish them. **Royal Thai Cuisine** at Chaweng is one recommen-dation. For nightlife, the thatched and open-sided **Reggae Pub** at Chaweng is highly rated by disco fans.
Phuket: Good restaurants plentiful in most major tourist areas. **Kan Eang 1 and 2** at Chalong Bay (tel 216-288, 216-726) are sister restau-rants. Inexpensive seafood is the speciality.
Songkhla: Best food is found along Nang Ngam Road, with, among other good eateries, the popular **Ran Ahaan Tae**.

PHUKET	J	F	M	A	M	J	J	A	S	O	N	D
AVERAGE TEMP. °F	82	84	85	85	83	83	82	82	81	81	82	81
AVERAGE TEMP. °C	28	29	29	30	29	28	28	28	27	27	28	28
Hours of Sun Daily	8	8	8	7	6	4	5	5	5	5	6	8
RAINFALL in	1	1	2	5	12	11	11	11	16	12	7	2
RAINFALL mm	30	21	49	121	319	259	291	272	399	309	176	59
Days of Rainfall	4	3	5	10	21	19	19	19	23	22	16	8

Travel Tips

Getting There

By air: Thailand is served by more than 50 international airlines. There are daily non-stop flights from major European cities to Bangkok; the flying time from London, for example, is about 12hr. Daily direct flights are also operated from Australia and the USA. As a Southeast Asian aviation hub, Bangkok is readily accessible from all main regional points.

By rail: Regular rail services link Bangkok with Singapore via Malaysia; the journey takes 34hr. The same route is also served by the ultra-deluxe – and ultra-expensive – Eastern & Oriental Express, a sister train to Europe's famous Orient Express, although without the latter's authentic heritage.

By road: Entry by road is possible from Malaysia, and you can also now drive to and from Laos via the Thai–Lao Friendship Bridge across the Mekong at Nong Khai. There are no vehicle crossing points between Thailand and Myanmar (Burma).

Airport tax

An airport tax of 200 baht for international flights and 20 baht for domestic services is charged for each passenger on departure.

Visas

For most nationalities, free tourist visas valid for 15 days are issued on arrival at Bangkok International Airport and other entry points. Visitors must possess a valid passport and ticket for onward travel. Available from Thai embassies and consulates overseas are **transit visas** (30–day stay), **tourist visas** (60–day stay) and **non-immigrant visas** (90–day stay). Applications must be accompanied by a photograph, appropriate fee and, for a non-immigrant visa, a letter of recommendation. Non-immigrant visas are difficult to obtain but 60–day tourist visas may be extended in Thailand for a further 30 days. It is essential that visitors who wish to leave Thailand and then return have a re-entry visa, obtainable in Bangkok from the Immigration Dept on Soi Suan Plu (allow 24hr). Visitors who overstay their visas are fined on departure at the rate of 100 baht per day.

Customs

Customs are generally painless. The declaration form you have to complete on arrival is little more than a formality unless you are carrying firearms, prohibited drugs, pornography or very large sums of money. Otherwise the usual camera, film, tobacco and alcohol allowances apply. There are standard green and red customs channels at Bangkok International Airport.

Health

No inoculations or vaccinations are required unless visitors have come from or passed through an infected area. As a general travel precaution, however, vaccination against **hepatitis A** is recommended, while it is also advisable to have a **tetanus** booster. Protection against **Japanese encephalitis** is a further consideration. Certain parts of Thailand are **malarial**

USEFUL PHRASES

Thai is a difficult language for Westerners to master. An attempt to learn just a few words can be useful, however, if only to win the appreciation – and amusement – of the Thais. Note: sentences take the suffix *khrap* if the speaker is male, and *kha* if female.

Hello/goodbye
　Sawaddee (khrap/kha)
Thank you
　Khawp khun (khrap/kha)
How are you?
　Sabai dee mai?
I'm fine
　Sabai dee
I don't feel well
　Mai sabai (khrap/kha)
No *Mai*
Yes *Chai* (it is),

or simply *khrap/kha*

What is your name?
　Khun cheu arai (khrap/kha)?
Where is? *You nai?*
How much? *Taw rai?*
Too expensive
　Paeng marg
I want to go to . . .
　Yaak pai . . .
Turn left *Leou sai*
Turn right *Leou khwa*
Straight ahead
　Trong pai
Stop here *Yoot tee nee*

Airplane *Kreung bin*
Airport *Sanam bin*
Bathroom *Hawng nam*
Boat *Reua*
Bus station *Sathanee rot meh*
Car *Rot*
Hospital *Rong phaya-bahn*

Hotel *Rawng ram*
Police station
　Sathanee tamruat
Post office *Prai-sannee*
Restaurant *Raan ahaan*
Side street *Soi*
Street *Thanon*
Taxi *Taksee*
Train station
　Sathanee rot fai

Hungry *Hew kao*
Thirsty *Hew nam*
Food *Ahaan*
Water *Nam*

Beef *Neua*
Chicken *Gai*
Coffee *Cafe*
Egg *Kai*
Fish *Plaa*
Fruit *Pohlamai*
Pork *Moo*
Rice *Khao*
Tea (hot) *Cha (rawn)*
Vegetables *Pahk*

Today *Wan nee*
Yesterday *Meua wan nee*
Tomorrow *Proong nee*

One	*Neung*
Two	*Song*
Three	*Sam*
Four	*See*
Five	*Haa*
Six	*Hok*
Seven	*Jet*
Eight	*Paet*
Nine	*Gaow*
Ten	*Sip*
Eleven	*Sip-et*
Twelve	*Sip song*
Twenty	*Yee sip*
Twenty-one	*Yee sip-et*
Twenty-two	*Yee sip song*
Thirty	*Sam sip*
One hundred	*Neung roi*
One thousand	*Neung phan*
Ten thousand	*Neung muen*

but the efficacy of prophylactics is questionable; should high fever occur within 14 days of a visit, consult a doctor. **Rabies** is prevalent in Thailand, so if you are bitten by an animal you should obtain medical treatment immediately. **Venereal diseases** can be easily contracted, but obviously there is an easy way of avoiding infection; the extent of **AIDS** is a cause for concern, so the same comment applies.

Other, less serious health hazards can be avoided by using common sense:
• don't stay too long in the sun
• don't drink tap water

• beware uncooked food
Generally, the standard of hospitals and health care in Bangkok and other major tourist centres is good and readily available. *

Personal Safety

In spite of Thailand having one of the world's highest murder rates, acts of violence are mostly limited to business disputes and affairs of the heart, and visitors have nothing to fear. Simple common-sense precautions – avoid touts, treat suspiciously friendly strangers with caution, do not flaunt wealth, etc. – should keep visitors out of trouble. A special Tourist

Police division has charge of visitor-related crime – for assistance in Bangkok call 221–6206, 281–5051 or 282–8129.

Clothing

Light, natural fabrics – for example, cotton – are best for staying cool. A sun hat is another extremely useful item to take with you.

Men should usually wear a suit and tie for business; however, as a concession to the climate, going in tie and shirtsleeves is acceptable. Generally, Thais tend to dress informally (mostly in Western style) but neatly, and prefer visitors to do likewise.

Respectable dress is required when visiting temples. Shoes should be removed whenever you enter a temple or a private home.

Accommodation

Bangkok and the main tourist centres offer a remarkable wealth of accommodation in all categories, from 'best in the world' to budget. Overall standards of comfort, hospitality and service are high.

For details of recommended establishments, consult the 'At a Glance' section at the end of each chapter. Telephone numbers prefixed 'BKK Res.' there refer to Bangkok reservation offices.

Transport

Air: The national carrier, Thai Airways International (THAI), operates an extensive network of domestic routes. Fares are comparatively inexpensive and no destination is much more than an hour's flying time from Bangkok. The private domestic carrier Bangkok Airways has a small route network, notably serving the non-THAI destinations Ko Samui and Sukhothai.

Trains: Rail transport is generally good – it is reasonably cheap, clean and comfortable, and in most instances the trains are on time. There are three classes (1st, 2nd and 3rd), and both air-conditioned and fan-cooled carriages. One slight drawback is that you have to book your tickets in advance – at least a week in advance if you're planning to travel on one of the trunk routes.

Main routes are Bangkok–Chiang Mai, Bangkok–Ubol Rachathani, Bangkok–Nong Khai and Bangkok–Sungai Golok (on the Malaysian border). Especially recommended is the overnight Bangkok–Chiang Mai train with air-conditioned sleeper (1st or 2nd class). Bangkok's main railway station is Hualampong (tel 223–7010, 223–7020).

Buses: Long-distance ordinary and air-conditioned buses link Bangkok with virtually all main towns. Fares are cheap – and so is life, judging by the criminal way in which many drivers handle their vehicles; fatal accidents are tragically frequent. Note that the different bus stations in Bangkok serve different parts of the country. For details (air-conditioned services) call

- 391–2504 (eastern routes)
- 279–4484 (north and northeastern routes)
- 434–5558 (southern routes)

Songthaews: A typically Thai version of the minibus concept. The word literally means 'two rows' and refers to an open-back pickup truck with two lateral bench seats. The vehicles ply set routes in towns and between villages in rural areas.

Money

Thailand's **currency** is the baht, which is divided into 100 satang. The exchange rate is listed daily (except Monday) in the business sections of the *Bangkok Post* and *Nation* newspapers.

Banknotes are issued in denominations of 10 baht (brown, but gradually being withdrawn in favour of coins), 20 baht (green), 50 baht (blue), 100 baht (red), 500 baht (purple) and 1000 baht (grey). Coins in circulation are 25 satang and 50 satang (bronze) and 1 baht, 5 baht and 10 baht (silver). To confuse matters, 1 baht coins come in three different sizes.

Internationally recognized **credit cards** are widely accepted. Banking services are provided nationwide by Thai banks (Bangkok Bank and Thai Farmers Bank are the two largest financial institutions) and branches of some foreign banks: hours are Mon–Fri 08:30–15:30. There are also authorized **currency exchange counters** in tourist areas. Hotel cashiers will change money but usually at a poorer rate than that given by banks.

Tipping

Tipping is not a common practice outside major hotels and restaurants.

Office Hours

- Government office hours are Mon–Fri 08:30–12:00 and 13:00–16:30.
- Most private companies work a five-day week 08:30–17:00.
- Department stores and bigger shops are generally open seven days a week from 10:00 to between 18:00 and 21:00.
- Smaller shops usually open 08:00–20:00.

Time Difference

Thailand is 7hr ahead of GMT.

Communications

Post and telecommunication services in Thailand are mostly good, in spite of a shortage of telephone lines. The General Post Office on New Road in Bangkok offers international phone, fax, telex and cable services on a 24hr basis. International direct dial (IDD) telephoning and postal and fax facilities are available at most hotels.

Electricity

Electric current is 220 volts/50 cycles. Both round and flat two-pin plugs are used, so an adaptor is useful.

Etiquette

Thais are easy-going and tolerant in the main although, like everyone else, they appreciate good manners.

The head and the feet are regarded as, respectively, the highest and lowest parts of the body symbolically as well as physically, so touching or patting people on the head is considered insulting; similarly, it is extremely rude to point with your feet or to step over a reclining body.

Displays of anger, ill-temper or impatience are also considered rude behaviour and, besides, achieve absolutely nothing. More is accomplished with a smile, even if you feel the person you are dealing with deserves to be strangled. The common Thai catchphrase *mai pen rai*, meaning 'nothing matters', is

a useful working philosophy.

Respect should be shown at all times to the monarchy and to Buddhism. The subjects are not matters for idle discussion: *lèse-majesté* is an indictable crime in Thailand. Women are prohibited from touching a Buddhist monk and should avoid even standing too close.

Thais are correctly addressed by their first names, prefixed by the word *Khun*, the Thai equivalent of Mr, Mrs, Ms and Miss.

The correct form of greeting is the *wai*, a gesture in which the hands are placed together as in prayer and raised to the face with fingertips at eye-level, with the head inclined slightly forward. Thais don't expect foreigners to *wai* but appreciate it when they do.

Festivals and Holidays

The Thais take great pleasure in celebrating traditional festivals and other commemorative occasions, both religious and secular. Some have fixed dates while others follow the lunar calendar. Many festivals

are peculiar to specific regions (especially the North and Northeast), but the most important national celebrations are described below.

January 1 *New Year's Day*

February *Makha Bucha* – falling on the day of the full moon – is an important Buddhist holiday commemorating the occasion when 1250 disciples gathered spontaneously to hear the Buddha speak. The day of merit-making ends with candlelit processions around temples.

April 6 *Chakri Day* – a national holiday commemorating the founding of the Chakri dynasty.
April 13 *Songkran* – the Thai New Year. Essentially a religious holiday when lustral water is sprinkled on Buddha images, but also a boisterous affair in which water is thrown over one and all. Especially lively in Chiang Mai.

May *Ploughing Ceremony* – takes place at the Pramane Ground in Bangkok at the

CONVERSION CHART		
FROM	**TO**	**MULTIPLY BY**
millimetres	inches	0.0394
metres	yards	1.0936
metres	feet	3.281
kilometres	miles	0.6214
hectares	acres	2.471
litres	pints	1.760
kilograms	pounds	2.205
tonnes	tons	0.984

To convert °Celsius to °Fahrenheit: x 9 ÷ 5 + 32

GOOD READING

Boisselier, Jean, *The Heritage of Thai Sculpture*, Bangkok, 1987 (reprint).

Boisselier, Jean, *Thai Painting*, Tokyo, 1976.

Bruce, Helen, *Nine Temples of Bangkok*, Bangkok, 1960.

Coedes, G., *The Making of Southeast Asia*, Los Angeles, 1966.

Collis, Maurice, *Siamese White*, Bangkok, 1982 (reprint).

Copper, Robert and Nanthapa, *Culture Shock: Thailand*, Singapore, 1982.

Dhani Nivat, Prince, *A History of Buddhism in Siam*, Bangkok, 1965.

Diskul, M.C. Subhadradis, *Art in Thailand*, Bangkok, 1970.

Hall, D.G.E., *History of Southeast Asia*, London, 1968 (3rd edn).

Hollinger, Carol, *Mai Pen Rai*, Boston, 1977.

Hoskin, John, *Bangkok*, Singapore, 1986.

Lewis, Paul and Elaine, *Peoples of the Golden Triangle*, London, 1984.

Mulder, Niels, *Everyday Life in Thailand*, Bangkok.

Segaller, Dennis, *Thai Ways*, Bangkok, 1980

Segaller, Dennis, *More Thai Ways*, Bangkok, 1982

Van Beek, S., and Invernizzi Tettoni, L., *The Arts of Thailand*, Hong Kong, 1985.

Various authors, *Thailand in the 80s*, Bangkok, 1984.

Warren, W., and Invernizzi Tettoni, L., *Thai Style*, Bangkok, 1989.

Waugh, Alec, *Bangkok, The Story of a City*, Bangkok, 1987 (reprint).

Wray, Elizabeth *et al.*, *Ten Lives of the Buddha*, Tokyo, 1972.

Wyatt, David K., *Thailand: A Short History*, New Haven, 1984.

start of the planting season on a date set by Brahman priests. Presided over by His Majesty the King, the ceremony involves ritual ploughing by sacred oxen and the planting of specially blessed rice seeds. A prediction is made for the success of the year's harvest.

May *Visakha Bucha* – falling on the day of the full moon – is the most important festival in the Buddhist calendar and celebrates the day (in different years) on which the Buddha was born, achieved enlightenment and died. In the evening there are candlelit processions around temples throughout the country.

May 1 *Labour Day*, an official holiday.

May 5 *Coronation Day* – a holiday commemorating the present King.

July *Asantha Bucha* (sometimes referred to as Buddhist Lent) – falling in the day of the full moon – is the anniversary of the Buddha's first sermon to his first five disciples. It also marks the beginning of a three-month period of retreat for Buddhist monks.

August 12 *Birthday of her Majesty Queen Sirikit.*

October *Ok Phansa* – celebrating the Buddha's return to earth after spending one rains-retreat season preaching in heaven. It also marks the end of the rain's retreat and the beginning of Krathin, the traditional time for presenting new robes and other gifts to monks. In some parts of the country the end of the rainy season is further marked by boat races.

October 23 *Chulalongkorn Day*, the anniversary of the death of King Chulalongkorn, Rama V, one of Thailand's most revered monarchs.

November *Loy Krathong* – held on the night of the full moon – is Thailand's most enchanting festival. It pays homage to Mae Khongkha, goddess of rivers and waterways, and is celebrated throughout the country by floating krathongs (little lotus-shaped boats bearing offerings of flowers, a candle, incense and a coin) on rivers, canals and ponds.

November *Golden Mount Fair* – Bangkok's biggest temple fair – held at Wat Saket next to the Golden Mount.

December 5 *Birthday of His Majesty the King*. Public buildings are elaborately decorated and illuminated at night.

December 10 *Constitution Day*, a public holiday.

December 31 *New Year's Eve*, a public holiday.

INDEX